Better Homes and Gardens®

NEW
CROCKERY
COOKER

COOK BOOK

Our seal assures you that every recipe in the
New Crockery Cooker Cook Book
has been tested in the Better Homes and Gardens® Test Kitchen.
This means that each recipe is practical and
reliable, and meets our high standards of taste appeal.

BETTER HOMES AND GARDENS® BOOKS
Editor: Gerald M. Knox
Art Director: Ernest Shelton
Managing Editor: David A. Kirchner
Editorial Project Managers: James D. Blume, Marsha Jahns,
  Rosanne Weber Mattson, Mary Helen Schiltz

Department Head, Cook Books: Sharyl Heiken
Associate Department Heads: Sandra Granseth,
  Rosemary C. Hutchinson, Elizabeth Woolever
Senior Food Editors: Julia Malloy, Marcia Stanley, Joyce Trollope
Associate Food Editors: Linda Henry, Mary Major, Diana McMillen,
  Mary Jo Plutt, Maureen Powers, Martha Schiel,
  Linda Foley Woodrum
Test Kitchen: Director, Sharon Stilwell; Photo Studio Director,
  Janet Pittman; Home Economists: Lynn Blanchard, Jean Brekke,
  Kay Cargill, Marilyn Cornelius, Jennifer Darling,
  Maryellyn Krantz, Lynelle Munn, Dianna Nolin, Marge Steenson

Associate Art Directors: Linda Ford Vermie, Neoma Alt West,
  Randall Yontz
Assistant Art Directors: Lynda Haupert, Harijs Priekulis,
  Tom Wegner
Graphic Designers: Mike Burns, W. Blake Welch, Brian Wignall
Art Production: Director, John Berg; Associate, Joe Heuer;
  Office Manager, Emma Rediger

President, Book Group: Fred Stines
Vice President, General Manager: Jeramy Lanigan
Vice President, Retail Marketing: Jamie Martin
Vice President, Administrative Services: Rick Rundall

BETTER HOMES AND GARDENS® MAGAZINE
President, Magazine Group: James A. Autry
Vice President, Editorial Director: Doris Eby
Executive Director, Editorial Services: Duane L. Gregg
Food and Nutrition Editor: Nancy Byal

MEREDITH CORPORATE OFFICERS
Chairman of the Board: E. T. Meredith III
President: Robert A. Burnett
Executive Vice President: Jack D. Rehm

NEW CROCKERY COOKER COOK BOOK
Editor: Linda Henry
Editorial Project Manager: James D. Blume
Graphic Designer: W. Blake Welch
Electronic Text Processor: Joyce Wasson
Food Stylists: Suzanne Finley, Pat Godsted, Janet Pittman
Contributing Photographers: M. Jensen Photography, Inc.,
  Scott Little, Tim Schultz Photography, Inc.
Contributing Writer: Sandra Mosley
Contributing Illustrator: Thomas Rosborough

On the front cover: Pork Stew with Cornmeal Dumplings
(see recipe, page 41)

Before starting this cook book, I spent much of my hour commute home each day thinking about what I could fix for supper. Each evening as I left the parking lot, I mentally scoured my favorite cook books for recipe ideas. Then, the inevitable question: Did I have the ingredients at home? Unless I felt like fighting the after-work crowds at the grocery store, my suppertime selections became pretty limited.

The *New Crockery Cooker Cook Book*, it seemed to me, was a chance to help myself and *all* absentee cooks who ponder the same questions. With its all-day cooking feature, the crockery cooker is a great appliance for me and many others. But beyond family favorites like pot roast and chili, I wondered, what other foods would convert to crockery cooking. Could I come up with dozens of great-tasting recipes for this appliance? The answer is a resounding YES. Recipes such as Chicken and Sausage Gumbo and Herbed Round Steak are only a sample of the variety you'll find.

So now my drive home is more pleasant because I *know* what's for supper—it's been cooking in my crockery cooker all day.

Linda J Henry

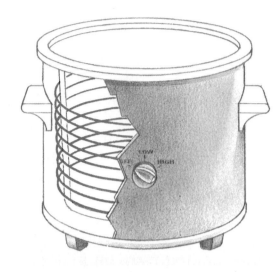

THE REST OF THE MEAL 61

*Baked vegetables, steamed breads and puddings,
and simmered desserts that turn your crockery cooker
into an oven.*

BEVERAGES 73

*Easy-to-serve hot drinks guaranteed to warm up any
party or cool day.*

CROCKERY-COOKER KNOW-HOW

With a crockery cooker and the *New Crockery Cooker Cook Book,* it's easy to work home-style meals into your busy life-style.

Each of our crockery-cooker recipes can be cooked either all day or about half of the day without any attention.

If you're going to be away from home all day, select the low-heat setting on the cooker. This lets you simmer the food for 10 to 12 hours.

For afternoons when you're running errands or attending meetings, or for those times when you're entertaining and want to get the food preparation done early, use the high-heat setting. It will cook the food in 5 to 6 hours.

TYPES OF CROCKERY COOKERS

Crockery cookers range in size from 1 to 6 quarts. We tailored the recipes in this book to fit three general sizes of cookers: 5- or 6-quart, 3½- or 4-quart, and

1-quart. The midsize crockery cookers are most common. Unless otherwise specified, the ingredient amounts and directions in our main recipes are suitable for both the midsize cookers and the large cookers. When special amounts or directions are necessary for the large cookers, you'll find that information listed directly below the main recipe. Ingredient amounts and directions for the 1-quart cookers are always listed separately.

Besides different sizes of cookers, there also are two different types (see illustrations, opposite). Recipes for this book were tested *only* in the type shown in Illustration A.

TIPS FOR USE

● *Illustration A:* This type of cooker has very low wattage; the elements or coils are on continuously.

You can identify this crockery cooker by the fixed settings on the heat control: low, high, and sometimes automatic (shifts from high to low heat).

These cookers have the continuous *slow* cooking needed for the recipes in this book.

● *Illustration B:* This type of cooker has a dial indicating temperatures in degrees. The heating element cycles on and off. Our recipes will not work in these cookers.

Crockery cookers are simple appliances to operate. The following general hints will help you use your crockery cooker more efficiently. (To learn about the specific features of your model, check the manufacturer's instruction booklet.)

● Do some of the chopping and measuring of ingredients ahead if possible (see tip, page 8). Assemble the ingredients in a bowl, cover, and refrigerate till it's time to begin cooking. If your cooker has a *removable liner,* assemble and refrigerate the food in the liner rather than a bowl.

● Keep the lid securely on the crockery cooker during cooking and be sure the food doesn't push up on the lid. Because crockery cooking depends on the heat that builds up in the container itself, resist the temptation to take a quick peek or stir frequently.

● To protect the crockery liner, avoid subjecting it to sudden temperature changes. For instance, do not preheat the cooker and then add food.

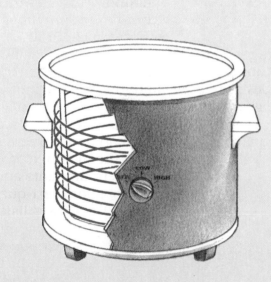

Illustration A: The heating coils wrap around the sides of the cooker. The crockery liner may or may not be removable.

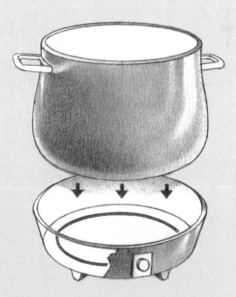

Illustration B: The heating coil is below the container.

● As soon as possible, transfer any leftover food to a storage container and refrigerate or freeze.
● Before using your crockery-cooker liner in your oven or microwave oven, check the manufacturer's directions.

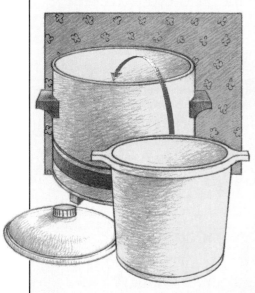

USING A TIMER

For extra convenience, use an automatic timer to start the cooker while you're away. The food, however, *should not stand more than two hours* before the cooker switches on.
● First, assemble the recipe and *thoroughly chill* it.
● When it's time to leave the house, place the food in the cooker. Plug the cooker into the timer, set the timer, and turn on the cooker.
● If a recipe includes frozen fish or chicken, do not use an automatic timer. The standing time would give the frozen food a chance to thaw, resulting in overcooked fish or chicken.

CLEANING

As soon as you remove the food from the crockery cooker, unplug it and fill the liner with hot soapy water (do not add cold water when the crockery liner is hot). Let the liner soak while you're eating. *Never immerse the cooker or cord in water.*
● Be careful during cleaning not to hit the crockery liner on the faucets or hard surfaces of your sink. Crockery chips easily.
● If soaking does not remove all the food residue, use a sponge, cloth, plastic cleaning pad, or nonabrasive cleaner to clean the crockery liner.
● If your cooker has a removable crockery liner, wash it, after soaking, in a dishwasher or by hand.
● For a cooker with a *nonremovable* crockery liner, wipe the liner clean with a dishcloth and soapy water after soaking. Rinse carefully and wipe dry.
● Both glass and plastic cooker lids are dishwasher safe, but be sure to put plastic lids only on the top rack of your dishwasher.
● Wipe the outside of the cooker's metal shell with a damp soft cloth and dry it with a towel.

MAKE-AHEAD TIP

Starting your crockery dinner before you leave in the morning will be easier if you follow this schedule and do some or all of the preparation the day before.

Prepare the meat: Brown the meat, drain well, and wrap in foil.

Prepare the vegetables: Clean and chop vegetables.

Chill overnight: Place the vegetables, seasonings, and liquids into a bowl or the crockery liner if it is removable (see illustration, above). Chill vegetables and meat.

MAIN DISHES

Explore the world of crockery cooking with Spaghetti Sauce Italiano, Sweet 'n' Sour Chicken, Curried Beef with Fruit, Greek-Style Stuffed Squash, and Choucroute Garni. Or try our versions of the old favorites, from pot roasts and meat loaf to barbecue-style ribs and corned beef.

Meat for Your Cooker

Your crockery cooker is great for cooking less expensive cuts of meat— beef chuck pot roasts, brisket, and pork shoulder roasts—because the long cooking at low heat tenderizes the meat. The low temperature also keeps the meat from shrinking as much as it does during other cooking methods.

For recipes that call for small cuts of meat (especially recipes reduced to fit into 1-quart cookers), keep your eyes peeled for specials at the meat counter. When meat is on sale, it's usually sold in large pieces. Buy these cuts and divide them into several smaller portions. Wrap individually, label, and freeze for later use.

Also be on the lookout for packaged smaller cuts of meat. Many supermarkets are beginning to sell small roasts and pot roasts. If your store offers only large roasts, ask the butcher to cut a 1- to 1½-pound piece for you.

Why Freeze Chicken for the Cooker?

The chicken recipes in this book call for frozen chicken pieces. We found that freezing the chicken before placing it in the crockery cooker slows the cooking of the chicken and assures that it is tender but not overcooked when the rest of the foods are done.

At least a day before cooking a crockery chicken recipe, freeze the chicken. To reduce the calories and for better texture and appearance, we suggest pulling the skin from the chicken pieces before freezing them. Then arrange the pieces in a single layer on a baking sheet. (The single layer is important so the pieces can be handled individually once frozen.) Cover and freeze the chicken till firm. If you won't be using the frozen pieces right away, remove them from the baking sheet and seal them in a freezer bag.

Pot Roast Dinner

1 2½- to 3-pound beef chuck
    pot roast
1 tablespoon cooking oil
1½ cups tomato juice
¼ cup wine vinegar
2 teaspoons Worcestershire
    sauce
1 teaspoon sugar
½ teaspoon salt
½ teaspoon dried basil,
    crushed
½ teaspoon dried thyme,
    crushed
¼ teaspoon pepper
1 clove garlic, minced
6 carrots, quartered and cut
    into ½-inch pieces
6 boiling onions
¼ cup quick-cooking tapioca
    Mashed potatoes

● Trim fat from roast. If necessary, cut roast to fit into crockery cooker. In a skillet brown roast on all sides in hot oil. In a bowl combine tomato juice, vinegar, Worcestershire sauce, sugar, salt, basil, thyme, pepper, and garlic.

● In a 3½-, 4-, 5-, or 6-quart crockery cooker place carrots and onions. Sprinkle tapioca over vegetables. Place roast atop vegetables. Pour tomato mixture over roast. Cover; cook on low-heat setting for 10 to 12 hours or high-heat setting for 5 to 6 hours.

● Transfer meat and vegetables to a platter. Skim fat from gravy. Pass gravy with meat. Serve with mashed potatoes. Serves 6.

For 1-quart crockery cooker: Use *one ¾-pound* beef chuck pot roast; *1 tablespoon* cooking oil; *½ cup* tomato juice; *1 tablespoon* wine vinegar; *¾ teaspoon* Worcestershire sauce; *¼ teaspoon* sugar; *dash* salt; *⅛ teaspoon* dried basil, crushed; *⅛ teaspoon* dried thyme, crushed; *dash* pepper; *1 small clove* garlic, minced; *2* carrots, cut into ½-inch pieces; *2* boiling onions; *4 teaspoons* quick-cooking tapioca; and mashed potatoes. Prepare as above. Cook for 10 to 12 hours. Makes 2 servings.

Cutting the meat to fit
Slice the roast into halves or thirds so it will fit into the crockery cooker without pushing up the lid during cooking. The lid of the cooker makes a handy pattern to use for cutting.

When purchasing the meat, if you choose a thicker roast with a diameter close to that of the cooker, cutting may not be necessary.

Harvest Pot Roast with
Tomato-Wine Gravy

Harvest Pot Roast with Tomato-Wine Gravy

Autumn flavors and golden autumn colors.

1 2- to 2½-pound beef chuck pot roast
1 tablespoon cooking oil
2 medium turnips, peeled and cut into 1-inch pieces (2 cups)
3 medium carrots, cut into ½-inch pieces (1½ cups)
1 10¾-ounce can condensed tomato soup
¼ cup dry red wine *or* water
3 tablespoons quick-cooking tapioca
⅛ teaspoon ground allspice
⅛ teaspoon pepper
1 pound winter squash, peeled, seeded, and cut into thin wedges or 1½- to 2-inch pieces (2 cups)

● Trim fat from roast. If necessary, cut roast to fit into crockery cooker. In a large skillet brown roast on all sides in hot oil.

● Meanwhile, in a 3½-, 4-, 5-, or 6-quart crockery cooker place turnips, carrots, tomato soup, red wine or water, tapioca, allspice, and pepper; stir together. Place roast atop vegetables. Place squash atop roast. Cover; cook on low-heat setting for 10 to 12 hours or high-heat setting for 5 to 6 hours.

● Transfer roast and vegetables to a warm serving platter. Skim fat from gravy. Pass gravy with roast. Makes 6 servings.

For 1-quart crockery cooker: Use *one 1-pound* beef chuck pot roast, *1 tablespoon* cooking oil, *1 cup* turnip pieces, *¾ cup* carrot pieces, *half of a 10¾-ounce can (⅔ cup)* condensed tomato soup, *2 tablespoons* dry red wine *or* water, *4 teaspoons* quick-cooking tapioca, *dash* ground allspice, *dash* pepper, and *1 cup* winter squash pieces. Prepare as above. Cook for 10 to 12 hours. Makes 3 servings.

Rump Roast and Vegetables

Save time and keep valuable nutrients and fiber by leaving the potatoes unpeeled.

1 2- to 2½-pound boneless beef round rump, round tip, *or* chuck pot roast
2 tablespoons cooking oil
1½ pounds small potatoes (about 10) *or* medium potatoes (about 4), halved
2 medium carrots, cut into ½-inch pieces (1 cup)
1 small onion, sliced
1 10-ounce package frozen lima beans
1 bay leaf
2 tablespoons quick-cooking tapioca
1 10¾-ounce can condensed vegetable beef soup
¼ cup water
¼ teaspoon pepper

● If necessary, cut roast to fit into the crockery cooker. In a large skillet brown roast on all sides in hot oil. Meanwhile, in a 3½-, 4-, 5-, or 6-quart crockery cooker place potatoes, carrots, and onion. Add frozen beans and bay leaf. Sprinkle tapioca over vegetables. Place roast atop vegetables.

● In a medium bowl combine condensed soup, water, and pepper; pour over roast. Cover; cook on low-heat setting for 10 to 12 hours or on high-heat setting for 5 to 6 hours.

● To serve, discard bay leaf and remove any strings from roast. Arrange roast and vegetables on a warm serving platter. Skim fat from gravy. Spoon some of the gravy over roast; pass remaining gravy with roast and vegetables. Makes 6 servings.

For 1-quart crockery cooker: Omit potatoes and halve remaining ingredients. Prepare as above. Cook for 10 to 12 hours. Makes 2 or 3 servings.

Gingersnap Pot Roast

All you need to complete this German-style menu is dark rye bread and chilled applesauce.

1 2- to 2½-pound beef chuck
    pot roast
1 tablespoon cooking oil
1 cup water
8 gingersnaps, crumbled
2 tablespoons red wine
    vinegar
1 teaspoon instant beef
    bouillon granules
⅛ teaspoon ground red pepper
3 medium sweet potatoes,
    peeled and quartered
3 medium carrots *or* 2
    medium parsnips, cut
    into ½-inch pieces
1 bay leaf

● Trim fat from roast. If necessary, cut roast to fit into crockery cooker. In a large skillet brown roast on all sides in hot oil. Meanwhile, in a small bowl combine water, gingersnaps, vinegar, bouillon granules, and red pepper.

● In a 3½- or 4-quart crockery cooker place potatoes, carrots or parsnips, and bay leaf. Place meat atop vegetables. Pour gingersnap mixture over meat. Cover; cook on low-heat setting for 10 to 12 hours or on high-heat setting for 5 to 6 hours.

● Transfer meat and vegetables to a platter. Remove bay leaf. Skim fat from gravy; stir gravy to combine. Ladle gravy over roast and vegetables. Makes 6 servings.

For 5- or 6-quart crockery cooker: Use *one 2½- to 3-pound* beef chuck pot roast; *1 tablespoon* cooking oil; *1 cup* water; *8* gingersnaps, crumbled; *2 tablespoons* red wine vinegar; *1 teaspoon* instant beef bouillon granules; *⅛ teaspoon* ground red pepper; *4 medium* sweet potatoes, peeled and quartered; *4* carrots, sliced; and *1* bay leaf. Prepare as above. Makes 8 servings.

For 1-quart crockery cooker: Use *one ¾-pound* beef chuck pot roast; *1 tablespoon* cooking oil; *½ cup* water; *4* gingersnaps, crumbled; *1 tablespoon* red wine vinegar; *½ teaspoon* instant beef bouillon granules; *dash* ground red pepper; *2 medium* sweet potatoes, peeled and quartered; *1* carrot, sliced; and *1* bay leaf. Prepare as above. Cook for 10 to 12 hours. Serves 2.

Corned Beef and Cabbage

To serve corned beef brisket cut it across the grain into thin slices.

2 medium onions, sliced
1 2½- to 3-pound corned beef
    brisket
1 cup apple juice
¼ cup packed brown sugar
2 teaspoons finely shredded
    orange peel
2 teaspoons prepared
    mustard
6 whole cloves
6 small cabbage wedges

● Place onions in a 3½-, 4-, 5-, or 6-quart crockery cooker. Trim fat from brisket. If necessary, cut brisket to fit into cooker; place atop onions. In a bowl combine apple juice, sugar, orange peel, mustard, and cloves; pour over brisket. Place cabbage atop brisket. Cover; cook on low-heat setting for 10 to 12 hours or on high-heat setting for 5 to 6 hours. Makes 6 servings.

For 1-quart crockery cooker: Use *1 small* onion, sliced; *one 1-pound* corned beef brisket; *⅓ cup* apple juice; *1 tablespoon* brown sugar; *½ teaspoon* finely shredded orange peel; *½ teaspoon* prepared mustard; and *2* whole cloves. Prepare as above. Cook for 10 to 12 hours. Steam or boil *2* cabbage wedges on top of the range; serve with cooked brisket. Serves 2.

Beef Brisket with Barbecue Sauce

¾ cup water
¼ cup Worcestershire sauce
1 tablespoon vinegar
1 teaspoon instant beef
   bouillon granules
½ teaspoon dry mustard
½ teaspoon chili powder
¼ teaspoon ground red pepper
2 cloves garlic, minced
1 2½-pound fresh beef brisket
½ cup catsup
2 tablespoons brown sugar
2 tablespoons margarine
   or butter

● For cooking liquid, in a bowl combine water, Worcestershire sauce, vinegar, bouillon granules, mustard, chili powder, red pepper, and garlic; reserve ½ *cup* liquid for sauce. Trim fat from brisket. If necessary, cut brisket to fit into cooker; place in a 3½- or 4-quart crockery cooker. Pour remaining liquid over brisket.

● Cover; cook on low-heat setting for 10 to 12 hours or high-heat setting for 5 to 6 hours. For sauce, in a small saucepan combine ½ cup reserved liquid, catsup, brown sugar, and margarine. Heat through. Pass sauce with meat. Serves 6 to 8.

For 5- or 6-quart crockery cooker: Double cooking liquid ingredients, reserving ½ *cup* for sauce. Leave all other ingredient amounts the same. Prepare as above. Serves 6 to 8.

For 1-quart crockery cooker: Use ½ *cup* water; *2 tablespoons* Worcestershire sauce; *2 teaspoons* vinegar; ½ *teaspoon* instant beef bouillon granules; ¼ *teaspoon* dry mustard; ¼ *teaspoon* chili powder; ⅛ *teaspoon* ground red pepper; *1 clove* garlic, minced; *one 1-pound beef chuck pot roast;* ¼ *cup* reserved liquid; ¼ *cup* catsup; *1 tablespoon* brown sugar; and *1 tablespoon* margarine *or* butter. Prepare roast and sauce as above. Cook roast for 10 to 12 hours. Makes 3 servings.

Beef Brisket in Beer

1 3- to 4-pound fresh beef
   brisket
2 onions, thinly sliced and
   separated into rings
1 bay leaf
1 cup beer
¼ cup chili sauce
2 tablespoons brown sugar
½ teaspoon dried thyme,
   crushed
¼ teaspoon salt
¼ teaspoon pepper
1 clove garlic, minced
2 tablespoons cornstarch
2 tablespoons water

● Trim fat from brisket. If necessary, cut brisket to fit into cooker. In a 3½-, 4-, 5-, or 6-quart crockery cooker place onions, bay leaf, and brisket. Combine beer, chili sauce, sugar, thyme, salt, pepper, and garlic; pour over brisket. Cover; cook on low-heat setting for 10 to 12 hours or high-heat setting 5 to 6 hours.

● Transfer brisket and onions to a platter; keep warm. Discard bay leaf. For gravy, skim fat from cooking juices. Measure 2½ cups juices and place in a saucepan. Combine cornstarch and water; add to saucepan. Cook and stir till thick and bubbly; cook and stir 2 minutes more. Pass gravy with meat. Serves 10.

For 1-quart crockery cooker: Use *one 1-pound beef chuck pot roast; 1 medium* onion, sliced; *1* bay leaf; ⅓ *cup* beer; *1 table-spoon* chili sauce; *2 teaspoons* brown sugar; ¼ *teaspoon* dried thyme, crushed; ⅛ *teaspoon* salt; ⅛ *teaspoon* pepper; *1 clove* garlic, minced; ⅔ *cup* cooking juices; *2 teaspoons* cornstarch; and *1 tablespoon* water. Prepare roast and gravy as above. Cook roast for 10 to 12 hours. Makes 2 or 3 servings.

Vegetable-Stuffed Meat Loaf

Vegetable-Stuffed Meat Loaf

½ cup shredded carrot
½ cup shredded potato
1 tablespoon cooking oil
1 beaten egg
2 tablespoons milk
½ cup fine dry bread crumbs
3 tablespoons snipped parsley
½ teaspoon onion salt
¼ teaspoon garlic powder
¼ teaspoon pepper
1½ pounds lean ground beef
3 tablespoons catsup
1 teaspoon prepared mustard

● In a small skillet cook carrot and potato in hot oil till tender, stirring occasionally. In a medium mixing bowl combine egg and milk. Stir in bread crumbs, parsley, onion salt, garlic powder, and pepper. Add ground meat and mix well.

● Crisscross three 18x2-inch foil strips atop a sheet of waxed paper. In the center of the foil strips pat *half* of the meat mixture into a 5-inch circle. Spread carrot mixture on meat circle to within ½ inch of edges. On another sheet of waxed paper pat remaining meat mixture into a 6-inch circle. Invert atop the first circle. Remove paper. Press edges of meat to seal well. Bringing up foil strips, transfer meat to a 3½-, 4-, 5-, or 6-quart crockery cooker. Press meat away from sides of the cooker.

● Cover; cook on low-heat setting for 9½ to 11½ hours or on high-heat setting for 3½ to 4 hours. In a bowl combine catsup and mustard. Spread over meat. Cover; cook on low-heat or high-heat setting for 30 minutes more. Using the foil strips, transfer meat loaf to a platter; discard the foil strips. Serves 8.

1-quart crockery cooker: Not recommended.

Giving meat loaf a lift
Lifting meat loaf into and out of the crockery cooker is easy with foil handles.

Tear off three 18x2-inch strips of *heavy* foil or use regular foil folded to double thickness. Crisscross the foil strips in a spoke design on top of a large sheet of waxed paper. Shape the meat loaf in the center of the spoke.

Lift the ends of the foil strips to transfer the meat loaf to the cooker. Leave the strips under the meat during cooking. The foil strips will enable you to remove the cooked meat loaf without destroying its shape.

Herbed Round Steak

Makes a wonderfully rich gravy for ladling over the tender steak and noodles.

2 pounds beef round steak, cut ¾ inch thick
1 tablespoon cooking oil
1 medium onion, sliced
1 10¾-ounce can condensed cream of celery soup
½ teaspoon dried oregano, crushed
¼ teaspoon dried thyme, crushed
¼ teaspoon pepper
Hot cooked noodles

● Trim fat from round steak. Cut meat into serving-size portions. In a skillet brown meat on both sides in hot oil. Place onion in a 3½- or 4-quart crockery cooker; place meat atop onion. In a small bowl combine soup, oregano, thyme, and pepper; pour over meat.

● Cover; cook on low-heat setting for 10 to 12 hours or on high-heat setting for 4 to 5 hours. Serve over noodles. Serves 6.

For 5- or 6-quart crockery cooker: Use *3 pounds* beef round steak, cut ¾ inch thick; *1 tablespoon* cooking oil; *2 medium* onions, sliced; *two 10¾-ounce cans* condensed cream of celery soup; *1 teaspoon* dried oregano, crushed; *½ teaspoon* dried thyme, crushed; *½ teaspoon* pepper; and hot cooked noodles. Prepare as above. Makes 8 to 10 servings.

For 1-quart crockery cooker: Halve all ingredients. Prepare as above. Cook for 10 to 12 hours. Makes 3 servings.

Curried Beef with Fruit

Vary the amount of curry powder to suit your taste.

1 2-pound boneless beef chuck pot roast
½ cup chopped onion
1 tablespoon cooking oil
1 15¼-ounce can pineapple chunks (juice pack)
⅔ cup orange juice
2 tablespoons quick-cooking tapioca
2 to 3 teaspoons curry powder
1 teaspoon instant beef bouillon granules
¼ teaspoon pepper
1 bay leaf
1 16-ounce can unpeeled apricot halves (water pack), drained
Hot cooked rice
½ cup peanuts, coarsely chopped

● Trim fat from meat; cut meat into ¾-inch cubes. In a large skillet brown meat cubes and onion, half at a time, in hot oil. In a 3½- or 4-quart crockery cooker combine *undrained* pineapple, orange juice, tapioca, curry powder, bouillon granules, pepper, and bay leaf. Add meat and onion to cooker.

● Cover; cook on low-heat setting for 9½ to 11½ hours or on high-heat setting for 3½ to 4½ hours. Add drained apricots. Cover; cook on low- or high-heat setting for 30 minutes more. Serve over rice. Pass peanuts to sprinkle atop beef. Serves 6.

For 5- or 6-quart crockery cooker: Use *one 3-pound* boneless beef chuck pot roast; *¾ cup* chopped onion; *1 tablespoon* cooking oil; *one 15¼-ounce can* pineapple chunks (juice pack); *1 cup* orange juice; *3 tablespoons* quick-cooking tapioca; *3 to 4 teaspoons* curry powder; *1½ teaspoons* instant beef bouillon granules; *¼ teaspoon* pepper; *2 bay leaves*; *one 16-ounce can* unpeeled apricot halves (water pack), drained; hot cooked rice; and *¾ cup* peanuts, chopped. Prepare as above. Serves 9.

For 1-quart crockery cooker: Halve all ingredients. Prepare as above. Cook for 10 to 12 hours. Makes 3 servings.

Spaghetti Sauce Italiano

Our taste panel rated this a delicious, hearty spaghetti sauce.

½ pound ground beef
¼ pound bulk Italian sausage
½ cup chopped onion
1 clove garlic, minced
1 16-ounce can tomatoes, cut up
1 8-ounce can tomato sauce
1 4-ounce can chopped mushrooms, drained
½ cup chopped green pepper
2 tablespoons quick-cooking tapioca
1 bay leaf
½ teaspoon dried oregano, crushed
¼ teaspoon dried basil, crushed
⅛ teaspoon pepper
Dash salt
Hot cooked spaghetti

● In a skillet cook ground beef, sausage, onion, and garlic till meat is brown and onion is tender; drain off fat.

● Meanwhile, in a 3½- or 4-quart crockery cooker combine *un-drained* tomatoes, tomato sauce, mushrooms, green pepper, tapioca, bay leaf, oregano, basil, pepper, and salt. Stir in browned meat mixture.

● Cover; cook on low-heat setting for 10 to 12 hours or high-heat setting for 5 to 6 hours. Remove bay leaf. Serve over hot spaghetti. Makes 4 or 5 servings.

For 5- or 6-quart crockery cooker: Double all ingredients. Prepare as above. Makes 8 to 10 servings.

For 1-quart crockery cooker: Omit bay leaf. Halve remaining ingredients. Prepare as above. Cook for 10 to 12 hours. Makes 2 or 3 servings.

Hot-and-Spicy Sloppy Joes

1½ pounds ground beef
1 large onion, chopped (1 cup)
1 clove garlic, minced
1 6-ounce can hot-style tomato juice *or* vegetable juice cocktail
½ cup catsup
½ cup water
2 tablespoons brown sugar
2 tablespoons chopped canned jalapeño peppers (optional)
1 tablespoon prepared mustard
2 teaspoons chili powder
1 teaspoon Worcestershire sauce
8 hamburger buns
Shredded cheddar cheese

● In a large skillet cook ground beef, onion, and garlic till meat is brown and onion is tender. Drain off fat.

● Meanwhile, in a 3½- or 4-quart crockery cooker combine tomato juice; catsup; water; brown sugar; jalapeño peppers, if desired; mustard; chili powder; and Worcestershire sauce. Stir in meat mixture. Cover; cook on low-heat setting for 10 to 12 hours or high-heat setting for 3 to 5 hours. Toast buns; spoon meat mixture over buns and sprinkle with cheese. Serves 8.

For 5- or 6-quart crockery cooker: Double all ingredients. Prepare as above. Makes 16 servings.

For 1-quart crockery cooker: Omit water. Use *1 pound* ground beef; *1 medium* onion, chopped; *1 small clove* garlic, minced; *one 6-ounce can* hot-style tomato juice; *¼ cup* catsup; *1 tablespoon* brown sugar; *1 tablespoon* chopped canned jalapeño peppers, if desired; *2 teaspoons* prepared mustard; *1 teaspoon* chili powder; *½ teaspoon* Worcestershire sauce; *4 or 5* hamburger buns; and shredded cheddar cheese. Prepare as above. Cook for 6 to 10 hours. Makes 4 or 5 servings.

Seeded Pork Roast

The seeds were a hit with our taste panel.

1   2½- to 3-pound pork
    sirloin roast
2   tablespoons soy sauce
1   tablespoon aniseed
1   tablespoon fennel seed
1   tablespoon caraway seed
1   tablespoon dillseed
1   tablespoon celery seed
1   teaspoon instant beef
    bouillon granules
1   cup water
    Apple wedges (optional)
    Mint sprigs (optional)

● Trim fat from roast. Rub soy sauce over surface of roast with fingers. On a large piece of foil combine aniseed, fennel seed, caraway seed, dillseed, and celery seed. Roll roast in seeds to coat evenly. Wrap roast in foil. Let meat stand in the refrigerator for 1 to 2 hours or overnight.

● Remove foil from roast. If necessary, cut roast to fit into the crockery cooker. Place roast in a 3½-, 4-, 5-, or 6-quart crockery cooker. In a small bowl dissolve bouillon granules in water; pour around roast. Cover; cook on low-heat setting for 10 to 12 hours or on high-heat setting for 5 to 6 hours.

● Transfer roast to a serving platter. Garnish platter with apple wedges and mint sprigs, if desired. Strain cooking juices; pass juices with roast. Makes 6 servings.

For 1-quart crockery cooker: Use *one 1-pound* pork sirloin roast, *1 tablespoon* soy sauce, *1 teaspoon* aniseed, *1 teaspoon* fennel seed, *1 teaspoon* caraway seed, *1 teaspoon* dillseed, *1 teaspoon* celery seed, *½ teaspoon* instant beef bouillon granules, and *⅓ cup* water. Prepare as above. Cook for 10 to 12 hours. Makes 2 or 3 servings.

Curried Pork Dinner

Add a tossed salad, peas, and hard rolls for an easy yet special guest menu.

1   2-pound boneless pork
    shoulder roast
2   tablespoons cooking oil
¼   cup quick-cooking tapioca
2   cups water
2   medium cooking apples,
    cored and cut into
    quarters
1   cup chopped onion
½   cup raisins
2   tablespoons curry powder
1   tablespoon instant chicken
    bouillon granules
½   teaspoon paprika
    Hot cooked rice

● Trim fat from roast; cut pork into 1-inch cubes. In a large skillet brown pork, half at a time, in hot oil. Transfer pork to a 3½- or 4-quart crockery cooker; sprinkle with tapioca. Add water, apples, onion, raisins, curry, bouillon granules, and paprika.

● Cover; cook on low-heat setting for 10 to 12 hours or on high-heat setting for 5 to 6 hours. Serve over rice. Serves 6.

For 5- or 6-quart crockery cooker: Use *one 3-pound* boneless pork shoulder roast; *3 tablespoons* cooking oil; *⅓ cup* quick-cooking tapioca; *3 cups* water; *3 medium* cooking apples, cored and quartered; *1⅓ cups* chopped onion; *⅔ cup* raisins; *3 tablespoons* curry powder; *4 teaspoons* instant chicken bouillon granules; *½ teaspoon* paprika; and hot cooked rice. Prepare as above. Makes 8 to 10 servings.

For 1-quart crockery cooker: Halve all ingredients. Prepare as above. Cook for 10 to 12 hours. Makes 3 servings.

Seeded Pork Roast

Apple Pork Roast and Vegetables

A splash of apple juice and a hint of cinnamon flavor the roast, vegetables, and gravy.

1   1½- to 2-pound pork
    shoulder roast
1   tablespoon cooking oil
3   medium parsnips, cut into
    ½-inch pieces (3 cups)
3   medium carrots, cut into
    bite-size sticks (1½ cups)
1   large green pepper, cut into
    wedges
2   stalks celery, cut into
    ½-inch pieces (1 cup)
3   tablespoons quick-cooking
    tapioca
1   6-ounce can frozen apple
    juice concentrate, thawed
¼   cup dry white wine
1   teaspoon instant beef
    bouillon granules
¼   teaspoon salt
¼   teaspoon ground cinnamon

● Trim fat from roast. If necessary, cut roast to fit into crockery cooker. In a large skillet brown roast on all sides in hot oil.

● Meanwhile, in a 3½-, 4-, 5-, or 6-quart crockery cooker place parsnips, carrots, green pepper wedges, and celery. Sprinkle with tapioca. Add apple juice concentrate, wine, beef bouillon granules, salt, cinnamon, and ¼ teaspoon *pepper.* Place roast atop vegetable mixture.

● Cover; cook on low-heat setting for 10 to 12 hours or high-heat setting for 5 to 6 hours. Makes 6 servings.

For 1-quart crockery cooker: Use *one ¾-pound* pork shoulder roast; *1 tablespoon* cooking oil; *1* parsnip *or 1* carrot, cut into bite-size sticks; *1 small* green pepper, cut into wedges; *1 stalk* celery, cut into ½-inch pieces; *5 teaspoons* quick-cooking tapioca; *⅓ cup* apple juice concentrate, thawed; *2 tablespoons* dry white wine; *½ teaspoon* instant beef bouillon granules; *⅛ teaspoon* salt; *⅛ teaspoon* ground cinnamon; and *⅛ teaspoon pepper.* Prepare as above. Cook for 10 to 12 hours. Serves 2 or 3.

**Layering foods for
best results**
Follow these steps for successful crockery cooking. First, place the vegetables in the bottom of the cooker. The liquid at the cooker bottom will help the vegetables cook and give them flavor.

Next, sprinkle quick-cooking tapioca over the vegetables. The tapioca will thicken the juices as the meal cooks, making a delicious, ready-to-serve gravy.

Finally, set the meat atop the vegetables and place the lid on the cooker securely.

Five-Spice Pork Roast

Five-spice powder is a blend of cinnamon, aniseed, fennel seed, pepper, and cloves.

1 2½- to 3-pound pork
   shoulder roast
1½ teaspoons five-spice powder
1 tablespoon cooking oil
¾ cup apple juice
⅓ cup dry white wine
2 tablespoons soy sauce
3 tablespoons cornstarch
2 tablespoons cold water
   Hot cooked rice

● Trim fat from roast. If necessary, cut roast or remove bone to fit roast into crockery cooker. Rub roast with five-spice powder. In a skillet brown roast on all sides in hot oil. Place roast in a 3½-, 4-, 5-, or 6-quart crockery cooker. Stir together apple juice, wine, and soy sauce. Pour over roast.

● Cover; cook on low-heat setting for 10 to 12 hours or on high-heat setting for 4½ to 5 hours. Remove roast; keep warm.

● For gravy, strain cooking liquid into a large glass measure. Skim off fat. Measure 2 cups liquid (if necessary, add water); pour into a saucepan. Combine cornstarch and water; add to saucepan. Cook and stir until thick and bubbly. Cook and stir 2 minutes more. Serve roast and gravy with rice. Serves 4 to 6.

For 1-quart crockery cooker: Use *one 1½-pound* pork shoulder roast, *¾ teaspoon* five-spice powder, *1 tablespoon* cooking oil, *⅓ cup* apple juice, *3 tablespoons* dry white wine, *1 tablespoon* soy sauce, *¾ cup* cooking liquid, *1 tablespoon* cornstarch, *1 tablespoon* cold water, and hot cooked rice. Prepare roast and gravy as above. Cook roast for 10 to 12 hours. Makes 2 or 3 servings.

Country Ribs

Complete the menu with baked beans, coleslaw, and cherry cobbler.

1 large onion, sliced and
   separated into rings
2½ to 3 pounds pork country-
   style ribs
1½ cups vegetable juice cocktail
½ of a 6-ounce can (⅓ cup)
   tomato paste
¼ cup molasses
3 tablespoons vinegar
1 teaspoon dry mustard
¼ teaspoon salt
¼ teaspoon pepper
⅛ teaspoon dried thyme,
   crushed
⅛ teaspoon dried rosemary,
   crushed

● In a 3½-, 4-, 5-, or 6-quart crockery cooker place onion rings. Place ribs atop onion. Combine vegetable juice cocktail, tomato paste, molasses, vinegar, dry mustard, salt, pepper, thyme, and rosemary. Reserve *1 cup* for sauce; cover and refrigerate. Pour remaining mixture over ribs. Cover; cook on low-heat setting for 10 to 12 hours or on high-heat setting for 5 to 6 hours.

● For sauce, in a small saucepan simmer reserved mixture, uncovered, for 10 minutes. Drain ribs; discard cooking liquid. Serve sauce with ribs. Makes 4 to 6 servings.

For 1-quart crockery cooker: Use *1 small* onion, sliced; *1 pound* pork country-style ribs; *¾ cup* vegetable juice cocktail; *3 tablespoons* tomato paste; *2 tablespoons* molasses; *4 teaspoons* vinegar; *½ teaspoon* dry mustard; *⅛ teaspoon* salt; *⅛ teaspoon* pepper; *pinch* dried thyme, crushed; and *pinch* dried rosemary, crushed. Reserve *½ cup* tomato mixture for sauce. Prepare ribs and sauce as above. Cook ribs for 5½ to 10 hours. Serves 2 or 3.

Italian-Sausage Heros

Italian-Sausage Heros

The high-heat setting is not recommended for this thick sandwich filling.

1 pound bulk Italian sausage
½ pound ground beef
1 cup chopped onion
1 15-ounce can tomato sauce
1 7½-ounce can tomatoes,
　cut up
1 4-ounce can mushroom
　stems and pieces, drained
½ cup sliced pitted ripe olives
4 teaspoons quick-cooking
　tapioca
1 teaspoon sugar
1 teaspoon dried oregano,
　crushed
⅛ teaspoon pepper
　Dash garlic powder
8 French-style rolls, split
　lengthwise
6 ounces sliced mozzarella
　cheese

● In a large skillet cook sausage, ground beef, and onion till meat is brown and onion is tender. Drain off fat.

● Meanwhile, in a 3½- or 4-quart crockery cooker combine tomato sauce, *undrained* tomatoes, mushrooms, olives, tapioca, sugar, oregano, pepper, and garlic powder. Stir in meat mixture. Cover; cook on low-heat setting for 10 to 12 hours.

● Using a fork, hollow out bottom halves of rolls, leaving ¼-inch-thick shells. (Reserve bread pieces for another use.) Place cheese in bottom halves, trimming as necessary to fit. Spoon meat mixture into rolls. Cut remaining cheese into strips and place atop meat mixture. Cover with bun tops. Serves 8.

For 5- or 6-quart crockery cooker: Double all ingredients. Prepare as above. Makes 16 servings.

For 1-quart crockery cooker: Leave the tomato amount at *one 7½-ounce can* tomatoes and halve remaining ingredients. Prepare as above. Cook for 10 to 12 hours. Makes 4 servings.

Barbecue-Style Pork Sandwiches

Pile coleslaw on the sandwiches or serve it on the side.

2 large green peppers, cut into
　strips (2½ cups)
1 large onion, thinly sliced and
　separated into rings
　(1 cup)
2 tablespoons quick-cooking
　tapioca
1 2½- to 3-pound pork
　shoulder roast
1 10¾-ounce can condensed
　tomato soup
2 tablespoons steak sauce
3 to 4 teaspoons chili powder
½ teaspoon sugar
¼ teaspoon garlic powder
¼ teaspoon pepper
　Several dashes bottled hot
　pepper sauce
6 kaiser rolls, split
　Coleslaw, drained (optional)

● In a 3½-, 4-, 5-, or 6-quart crockery cooker combine green pepper strips and onion rings. Sprinkle tapioca over vegetables. Trim fat from roast. If necessary, cut roast to fit into cooker. Place roast atop vegetables.

● For barbecue sauce, in a medium bowl combine tomato soup, steak sauce, chili powder, sugar, garlic powder, pepper, and hot pepper sauce. Pour over roast.

● Cover; cook on low-heat setting for 10 to 12 hours or on high-heat setting for 5 to 6 hours. Remove roast from cooker and thinly slice or shred meat. Skim fat from sauce.

● Serve meat on kaiser rolls; top with barbecue sauce and coleslaw, if desired. Makes 6 servings.

For 1-quart crockery cooker: Halve all ingredients. Prepare as above. Cook for 10 to 12 hours. Makes 3 servings.

Choucroute Garnie

Choucroute Garnie: pronunciation, shoo-kroot gar-nee; translation, sauerkraut and meat.

2 small cooking apples
2 fully cooked knackwurst
2 medium potatoes, quartered
2 medium carrots, cut into
   ½-inch pieces (1 cup)
½ cup chopped onion
3 juniper berries, crushed
   (optional)
1 bay leaf
2 medium smoked pork loin
   chops, cut ¾ inch thick,
   or ½ pound fully cooked
   ham slice, cut into pieces
1 16-ounce can sauerkraut,
   drained
½ cup water
½ cup dry white wine
1 teaspoon instant chicken
   bouillon granules
⅛ teaspoon ground cloves
⅛ teaspoon pepper

● Core apples and cut into quarters. Score knackwurst diagonally. In a 3½- or 4-quart crockery cooker place potatoes; carrots; onion; juniper berries, if desired; bay leaf; pork chops or ham; sauerkraut; apples; and knackwurst. Combine water, wine, bouillon granules, cloves, and pepper; add to cooker.

● Cover; cook on low-heat setting for 10 to 12 hours or on high-heat setting for 4½ to 5 hours. Discard bay leaf. Serves 4.

For 5- or 6-quart crockery cooker: Use *3* cooking apples; *3* fully cooked knackwurst; *3* potatoes, quartered; *3* carrots, cut into ½-inch pieces; *¾ cup* chopped onion; *5* juniper berries, crushed (optional); *2* bay leaves; *3 medium* smoked pork loin chops, cut ¾ inch thick, *or ¾ pound* fully cooked ham slice, cut into pieces; *one 27-ounce can* sauerkraut, drained; *¾ cup* water; *¾ cup* dry white wine; *1½ teaspoons* instant chicken bouillon granules; *⅛ teaspoon* ground cloves; and *¼ teaspoon* pepper. Prepare as above. Makes 6 servings.

For 1-quart crockery cooker: Halve all ingredients. Prepare as above. Cook for 6 to 10 hours. Makes 2 servings.

Pork Chops with Mushroom Sauce

4 pork loin chops, cut ¾ inch
   thick
1 tablespoon cooking oil
1 small onion, thinly sliced
1 10¾-ounce can condensed
   cream of mushroom soup
¾ cup dry white wine
1 4-ounce can sliced
   mushrooms, drained
2 tablespoons quick-cooking
   tapioca
2 teaspoons Worcestershire
   sauce
1 teaspoon instant beef
   bouillon granules
¾ teaspoon dried thyme,
   crushed
¼ teaspoon garlic powder
   Hot cooked rice

● In a skillet brown chops on both sides in hot oil. In a 3½- or 4-quart crockery cooker place onion; add chops. In a bowl combine soup, wine, mushrooms, tapioca, Worcestershire sauce, bouillon granules, thyme, and garlic powder; pour over chops.

● Cover; cook on low-heat setting for 10 to 12 hours or on high-heat setting for 4½ to 5 hours. Serve over rice. Serves 4.

For 5- or 6-quart crockery cooker: Use *6* pork chops, cut ¾ inch thick. Leave remaining ingredient amounts the same. Prepare as above. Makes 6 servings.

For 1-quart crockery cooker: Use *2* pork chops, cut ¾ inch thick; *2 teaspoons* cooking oil; *1 small* onion, sliced; *half of a 10¾-ounce can* condensed cream of mushroom soup; *⅓ cup* dry white wine; *one 2½-ounce jar* sliced mushrooms, drained; *1 tablespoon* quick-cooking tapioca; *1 teaspoon* Worcestershire sauce; *½ teaspoon* instant beef bouillon granules; *¼ teaspoon* dried thyme, crushed; *⅛ teaspoon* garlic powder; and hot cooked rice. Prepare as above. Cook for 10 to 12 hours. Serves 2.

Chicken and Sausage Cassoulet

Cassoulet (kas-uh-LAY)—a casserole of beans, herbs, and meat—tastes as good as it sounds.

1 15-ounce can navy beans
1 cup tomato juice
2 medium carrots, cut into
   ½-inch pieces (1 cup)
1 stalk celery, cut into
   ½-inch pieces (½ cup)
½ cup chopped onion
1 clove garlic, minced
1 bay leaf
1 teaspoon instant chicken
   bouillon granules
½ teaspoon dried basil,
   crushed
½ teaspoon dried oregano,
   crushed
4 chicken drumsticks,
   skinned and frozen
4 ounces smoked turkey
   sausage link

● In a 3½- or 4-quart crockery cooker combine *undrained* beans, tomato juice, carrots, celery, onion, garlic, bay leaf, bouillon granules, basil, and oregano.

● Place *frozen* chicken atop bean mixture. Cut sausage in half lengthwise and slice. Place atop chicken.

● Cover; cook on low-heat setting for 10 to 12 hours or high-heat setting for 5 to 6 hours. Remove bay leaf. Makes 4 servings.

For 5- or 6-quart crockery cooker: Double all ingredients. Prepare as above. Makes 8 servings.

For 1-quart crockery cooker: Halve all ingredients. Prepare as above. Cook for 10 to 12 hours. Makes 2 servings.

Sweet 'n' Sour Chicken

Choose your favorite meaty chicken pieces: breasts, thighs, or drumsticks.

3 medium carrots, cut into
   ¼-inch pieces (1½ cups)
1 large green pepper, cut
   into 1-inch pieces
1 medium onion, cut into
   wedges
2 tablespoons quick-cooking
   tapioca
2½ to 3 pounds meaty chicken
   pieces, skinned and frozen
1 8-ounce can pineapple
   chunks (juice pack)
⅓ cup packed brown sugar
⅓ cup red wine vinegar
1 tablespoon soy sauce
½ teaspoon instant chicken
   bouillon granules
¼ teaspoon garlic powder
¼ teaspoon ground ginger
   Hot cooked rice

● In a 3½-, 4-, 5 , or 6-quart crockery cooker combine carrots, green pepper, and onion. Sprinkle tapioca over vegetables. Place *frozen* chicken pieces atop vegetables. For sauce, in a small bowl combine *undrained* pineapple, brown sugar, vinegar, soy sauce, bouillon granules, garlic powder, and ginger. Pour sauce over chicken pieces.

● Cover; cook on low-heat setting for 10 to 12 hours or on high-heat setting for 5 to 6 hours. Serve over rice. Makes 6 servings.

For 1-quart crockery cooker: Use *1 small* carrot, cut into ¼-inch pieces; *½ small* green pepper, cut into 1-inch pieces; *¼ cup chopped* onion; *2 teaspoons* quick-cooking tapioca; *¾ pound chicken thighs*, skinned and *frozen; 3 tablespoons unsweetened pineapple juice or water; 2 tablespoons* brown sugar; *2 tablespoons* red wine vinegar; *1 teaspoon* soy sauce; *¼ teaspoon* instant chicken bouillon granules; *dash* garlic powder; *dash* ground ginger; and hot cooked rice. Prepare as above. Cook for 9 to 10 hours. Makes 2 servings.

Paella

It takes only a touch of saffron or turmeric to flavor the whole dish.

2 medium carrots, cut into
   ½-inch pieces (1 cup)
1 large onion, coarsely
   chopped (1 cup)
1 bay leaf
2 pounds chicken thighs and
   drumsticks, skinned and
   frozen
1 cup cubed fully cooked ham
1 16-ounce can stewed
   tomatoes
2 teaspoons instant chicken
   boullion granules
2 cloves garlic, minced
¼ teaspoon pepper
1 pound fresh or frozen
   shrimp in shells *or* 8
   ounces frozen cooked
   shrimp
1 cup fresh *or* frozen peas
2 cups water
1 cup long grain rice
   Pinch ground saffron *or* ⅛
   teaspoon ground turmeric

● In a 3½-, 4-, 5-, or 6-quart crockery cooker place carrots, onion, and bay leaf. Top with *frozen* chicken pieces and ham. In a bowl combine *undrained* tomatoes, bouillon granules, garlic, and pepper; add to cooker. Cover; cook on low-heat setting for 9½ to 11½ hours or on high-heat setting for 4½ to 5½ hours.

● Thaw shrimp, if frozen. Peel and devein shrimp in shells, leaving tail intact, if desired. Add shrimp and peas to the crockery cooker. Cook on low-heat setting for 30 minutes more or on high-heat setting for 20 minutes more.

● Meanwhile, in a medium saucepan combine water, rice, and saffron or turmeric. Bring to boiling; reduce heat. Cover and simmer for 15 minutes. Remove from heat. Let stand, covered, for 10 minutes. Fluff rice with a fork.

● To serve, remove bay leaf from chicken mixture. Serve chicken mixture with a slotted spoon over cooked rice mixture. Makes 6 servings.

For 1-quart crockery cooker: Halve all ingredients. Prepare chicken and rice mixtures as above. Cook chicken mixture for 9½ to 11½ hours. Add shrimp and peas. Cook for 30 minutes more. Makes 3 servings.

Italian Chicken Dinner

An easy family dinner.

1 small head cabbage, cut into
   wedges (about 1 pound)
1 medium onion, sliced and
   separated into rings
1 4-ounce can mushroom
   stems and pieces, drained
2 tablespoons quick-cooking
   tapioca
1 2½- to 3-pound broiler-fryer
   chicken, cut up, skinned,
   and frozen
1 15-ounce jar extra thick and
   spicy meatless spaghetti
   sauce
   Grated Parmesan cheese

● In a 3½-, 4-, 5-, or 6-quart crockery cooker place cabbage wedges, onion, and mushrooms. Sprinkle tapioca over vegetables. Place *frozen* chicken pieces atop vegetables. Pour spaghetti sauce over chicken.

● Cover; cook on low-heat setting for 10 to 12 hours or on high-heat setting for 4½ to 5½ hours. Transfer to a serving platter. Sprinkle with Parmesan cheese. Makes 6 servings.

For 1-quart crockery cooker: Use ¼ *small head* cabbage, cut into 2 wedges; ½ *small* onion, sliced and separated into rings; *one 2-ounce can* mushroom stems and pieces, drained; *4 teaspoons* quick-cooking tapioca; *½ pound meaty chicken pieces,* skinned and *frozen;* ¾ *cup* extra thick and spicy meatless spaghetti sauce; and grated Parmesan cheese. Prepare as above. Cook for 8 to 9 hours. Makes 1 or 2 servings.

Paella

Chicken Mole

Olé, olé, mole (MO-lay)! This spicy sauce with chilies and chocolate is magnifica.

1 7½-ounce can tomatoes
¾ cup chicken broth
½ cup chopped onion
¼ cup slivered almonds
1 to 2 canned jalapeño
     peppers, drained
3 tablespoons unsweetened
     cocoa powder
3 tablespoons raisins
1 tablespoon sesame seed
3 cloves garlic
1 teaspoon sugar
¼ teaspoon ground cinnamon
⅛ teaspoon ground nutmeg
⅛ teaspoon ground coriander
2 tablespoons quick-cooking
     tapioca
1 2½- to 3-pound broiler-fryer
     chicken, cut up, skinned,
     and frozen
   Hot cooked rice
2 tablespoons slivered
     almonds, toasted

● For mole sauce, in a blender container or food processor bowl combine *undrained* tomatoes, chicken broth, onion, ¼ cup almonds, jalapeño peppers, cocoa powder, raisins, sesame seed, garlic, sugar, cinnamon, nutmeg, and coriander. Cover and blend or process to a coarse puree.

● In a 3½-, 4-, 5-, or 6-quart crockery cooker place tapioca. Add *frozen* chicken and then sauce. Cover; cook on low-heat setting for 10 to 12 hours or on high-heat setting for 4½ to 5½ hours.

● Arrange chicken over rice on a platter. Skim fat from sauce; pour sauce over chicken. Sprinkle with almonds. Serves 6.

For 1-quart crockery cooker: Use *½ cup tomato juice; ⅓ cup* chicken broth; *¼ cup* chopped onion; *2 tablespoons* slivered almonds; *1 small* canned jalapeño pepper, drained; *2 teaspoons* unsweetened cocoa powder; *1 tablespoon* raisins; *2 teaspoons* sesame seed; *1 clove* garlic; *½ teaspoon* sugar; *⅛ teaspoon* ground cinnamon; *dash* ground nutmeg; *dash* ground coriander; *1 tablespoon* quick-cooking tapioca; *¾ pound chicken thighs,* skinned and *frozen;* hot cooked rice; and *1 tablespoon* slivered almonds, toasted. Prepare as above. Cook for 9 to 10 hours. Makes 2 servings.

Tangy Chicken

Lemon, pineapple, and orange give the chicken a pleasant tang.

1 6-ounce can frozen
     pineapple-orange juice
     concentrate, thawed
½ cup catsup
2 tablespoons lemon juice
2 tablespoons quick-cooking
     tapioca
2 inches stick cinnamon,
     broken
8 whole allspice
4 whole cloves
1 2½- to 3-pound broiler-
     fryer chicken, cut up,
     skinned, and frozen
   Hot cooked couscous

● For sauce, in a small bowl combine juice concentrate, catsup, and lemon juice. Pour about *half* of the sauce into a 3½- or 4-quart crockery cooker. Add tapioca to the cooker; stir. For spice bag, place cinnamon, allspice, and cloves in cheesecloth and tie (see tip, page 78). Add bag to cooker. Place *frozen* chicken pieces in crockery cooker. Pour remaining sauce over chicken.

● Cover; cook on low-heat setting for 10 to 12 hours or high-heat setting for 4½ to 5½ hours. Discard spice bag. Transfer chicken to a serving platter. Skim fat from sauce. Serve sauce and hot couscous with chicken. Makes 6 servings.

For 5- or 6-quart crockery cooker: Double all ingredients. Prepare as above. Makes 12 servings.

For 1-quart crockery cooker: Halve all ingredients. Prepare as above. Cook for 9 to 10 hours. Makes 2 or 3 servings.

Turkey Roast Chablis

The gravy has a mild wine flavor.

¾ cup dry white wine
½ cup chopped onion
1 clove garlic, minced
1 bay leaf
1 3- to 3½-pound frozen
   boneless turkey roast,
   thawed
1 teaspoon dried rosemary,
   crushed
¼ teaspoon pepper
⅓ cup light cream *or* milk
2 tablespoons cornstarch
⅛ teaspoon salt

● In a 3½-, 4-, 5-, or 6-quart crockery cooker combine white wine, onion, garlic, and bay leaf. If turkey roast is wrapped in netting, remove netting and discard. If gravy packet is present, remove packet from roast; refrigerate packet for another use. Combine rosemary and pepper. Rub roast with rosemary mixture. Place turkey roast in cooker.

● Cover; cook on low-heat setting for 10 to 12 hours or on high-heat setting for 4½ to 5½ hours. Remove roast and keep warm. For gravy, strain cooking juices; discard solids. Skim fat from juices. Measure 1⅓ cups juices into a small saucepan. Combine cream or milk, cornstarch, and salt; stir into juices. Cook and stir till thickened and bubbly. Cook and stir 2 minutes more.

● Slice turkey roast. Spoon some gravy over roast. Pass remaining gravy with roast. Makes 6 to 8 servings.

For 1-quart crockery cooker: Not recommended.

Barbecue-Style Turkey Thighs

Trim the turkey thighs, if necessary, before freezing them so they'll lie flat in the cooker. That way, they'll cook more evenly and have a richer barbecue flavor.

½ cup catsup
2 tablespoons brown sugar
1 tablespoon quick-cooking
   tapioca
1 tablespoon vinegar
1 teaspoon Worcestershire
   sauce
¼ teaspoon ground cinnamon
¼ teaspoon crushed red
   pepper
2 to 2½ pounds turkey thighs
   (about 2 thighs) *or* meaty
   chicken pieces (breasts,
   thighs, and drumsticks),
   skinned and frozen
   Hot cooked rice *or* noodles
   (optional)

● In a 3½- or 4-quart crockery cooker combine catsup, brown sugar, tapioca, vinegar, Worcestershire sauce, cinnamon, and red pepper. Place *frozen* turkey thighs or chicken pieces atop catsup mixture, meaty side down and flat in the cooker.

● Cover; cook on low-heat setting for 10 to 12 hours or high-heat setting for 5 to 6 hours. Serve turkey or chicken and sauce over rice or noodles, if desired. Makes 4 to 6 servings.

For 5- or 6-quart crockery cooker: Use *¾ cup* catsup, *3 tablespoons* brown sugar, *4 teaspoons* quick-cooking tapioca, *4 teaspoons* vinegar, *2 teaspoons* Worcestershire sauce, *¼ teaspoon* ground cinnamon, *¼ teaspoon* crushed red pepper, and *3 to 3½ pounds* turkey thighs *or* meaty chicken pieces, skinned and *frozen.* Prepare as above. Makes 6 to 8 servings.

For 1-quart crockery cooker: Use *1 pound* meaty chicken pieces, skinned and *frozen,* and halve remaining ingredients. Prepare as above. Cook for 9 to 10 hours. Makes 2 or 3 servings.

Greek-Style Stuffed Squash

Dinner served in individual shells.

½ pound ground lamb *or* beef
¼ cup chopped onion
¼ cup plain yogurt
2 tablespoons raisins
⅛ teaspoon salt
⅛ teaspoon ground cinnamon
⅛ teaspoon ground nutmeg
1 buttercup squash
Salt
¼ cup water
2 to 3 tablespoons crumbled feta cheese

● For meat filling, in a medium skillet cook lamb or beef and onion till meat is brown and onion is tender. Drain off fat. Stir in yogurt, raisins, salt, cinnamon, and nutmeg.

● Wash squash. Halve squash horizontally; remove seeds. Sprinkle lightly with salt. Spoon meat filling into squash cavities. Wrap each squash half tightly in foil.

● Pour water into a 3½-, 4-, 5-, or 6-quart crockery cooker. Stack squash halves, cut side up, in cooker. Cover; cook on low-heat setting for 10 to 12 hours or on high-heat setting for 4 to 5 hours. Unwrap and top with feta cheese. Makes 2 servings.

For 1-quart crockery cooker: Use ¼ *pound* ground lamb *or* beef, *2 tablespoons* chopped onion, *2 tablespoons* plain yogurt, *1 tablespoon* raisins, *dash* salt, *dash* ground cinnamon, *dash* ground nutmeg, *1 small acorn squash* (cut ½- to 1-inch slice off top; scoop out seeds), salt, ¼ *cup* water, and *1 tablespoon* crumbled feta cheese. Prepare as above. Cook for 8 to 10 hours. Makes 1 serving.

Middle-Eastern Sandwiches

An exotic mix of garlic, wine, allspice, mint, and yogurt flavors the lamb.

1½ pounds ground lamb *or* ground beef
1 cup chopped onion
4 cloves garlic, minced
1 15-ounce can garbanzo beans, drained
¾ cup dry red wine
½ of a 6-ounce can (⅓ cup) tomato paste
¼ cup water
½ teaspoon ground allspice
½ teaspoon dried mint, crushed
¼ teaspoon salt
¼ teaspoon pepper
6 small pita bread rounds
6 lettuce leaves
Thinly sliced cucumber
1 medium tomato, chopped
Plain yogurt

● In a skillet cook ground lamb or beef, onion, and garlic till meat is brown and onion is tender. Drain off fat.

● Meanwhile, in a 3½- or 4-quart crockery cooker combine garbanzo beans, wine, tomato paste, water, allspice, mint, salt, and pepper. Stir in meat mixture. Cover; cook on low-heat setting for 10 to 12 hours or on high-heat setting for 5 to 6 hours.

● To serve, make a slit at one end of each pita and open to form a large pocket. Line pitas with lettuce, cucumber, and tomato. Stir meat mixture. Spoon meat mixture and then yogurt into pitas. Makes 6 servings.

For 5- or 6-quart crockery cooker: Double all ingredients. Prepare as above. Makes 12 servings.

For 1-quart crockery cooker: Halve all ingredients. Prepare as above. Cook for 10 to 12 hours. Makes 3 servings.

SOUPS AND STEWS

Come home to the aroma of soup or stew simmering in your crockery cooker, just ready to ladle up for dinner. To complete the menu, choose one of the fast homemade bread or roll recipes included in this section.

Soup and Stew Tips

Convenient Substitutes

When a recipe calls for beef broth or chicken broth, you can, if you like, make homemade broth using your crockery cooker and one of the recipes on the opposite page.

But if you're in a hurry, don't despair. Excellent broth substitutes are available. And if you don't have the flavor specified in the recipe, use a different one—you may even prefer it!

Canned chicken and beef broth are ready to use straight from the can. Instant bouillon granules and cubes can be purchased in beef, chicken, vegetable, and onion flavors. One cube or 1 teaspoon granules mixed with 1 cup water makes an easy broth.

Top It Off

Heading our list of favorite soup toppings are crushed crackers, shredded cheese, toasted bread cubes or seasoned croutons, plain or cheese-flavored popcorn, shredded carrot, sour cream, and snipped parsley or chives.

Petite squares or triangles cut from toast (or more elaborate shapes cut with small cookie cutters) are fun to float on a soup. For extra flavor, spread the toast with flavored butter, cheese spread, or pesto before cutting.

Freezing Leftovers

Freeze any leftover soup or stew in freezer containers with tight-fitting lids. Because food expands when it freezes, leave about ½ inch of headspace below the rims of the containers.

Another convenient way to freeze soups and broths is to use plastic ice-cube trays. Simply cool the soup or broth and pour it into the individual sections of an ice-cube tray. Freeze till the soup is firm, pop out the cubes of frozen soup, seal them in a freezer bag, and return to the freezer.

When you're ready to eat, reheat a few cubes for a single serving or more cubes for the entire family.

Stewed Beef and Broth

Use this homemade broth to make flavorful soups and stews.

3 pounds meaty beef soup bones (beef shank crosscuts, short ribs, knuckle bones, *or* marrow bones)
1 tablespoon cooking oil
2 large onions, sliced
4 cloves garlic, halved
8 sprigs parsley
4 large bay leaves
8 whole black peppercorns
1½ teaspoons salt
5 cups water
1 egg white (optional)
1 eggshell, crushed (optional)
¼ cup water (optional)

● In a large skillet brown soup bones on all sides in hot oil. In a 3½-, 4-, 5-, or 6-quart crockery cooker combine onions, garlic, parsley, bay leaves, peppercorns, and salt. Add browned soup bones and 5 cups water. Cover; cook on low-heat setting for 10 to 12 hours or on high-heat setting for 5 to 6 hours.

● Remove bones from cooker. Strain broth through a large sieve or colander lined with 2 layers of cheesecloth. Discard solids. If desired, clarify broth by combining egg white, eggshell, and ¼ cup water in a large saucepan. Add hot broth. Bring to boiling; let stand 5 minutes. Strain broth.

● If using broth right away, skim off fat. *Or,* if storing broth for later use, chill in a bowl for 6 hours. Lift off fat. Pour broth into an airtight container, discarding the residue in the bottom of the bowl; seal. Chill up to 2 days or freeze up to 3 months.

● Remove meat from bones. Discard bones. Place meat in an airtight container; seal. Chill up to 3 days or freeze up to 3 months. Makes about 5 cups broth and 3 cups cooked meat.

For 1-quart crockery cooker: Not recommended.

Stewed Chicken and Broth

Use the broth or meat right away in a soup or main-dish recipe. Or, freeze the meat and broth in meal-size portions for later use.

1 4- to 4½-pound stewing, roasting, *or* broiler-fryer chicken, cut up
4 celery stalks with leaves, cut up
1 small onion, sliced
2 sprigs parsley
1 bay leaf
½ teaspoon salt
¼ teaspoon dried thyme, crushed
¼ teaspoon dried marjoram, crushed
¼ teaspoon celery salt
¼ teaspoon pepper
4 cups water

● In a 3½-, 4-, 5-, or 6-quart crockery cooker combine cut-up chicken, celery, onion, parsley, bay leaf, salt, thyme, marjoram, celery salt, and pepper. Add water. Cover; cook on low-heat setting for 8 to 10 hours or on high-heat setting for 4 to 5 hours.

● Remove chicken from cooker. Strain broth through a large sieve lined with 2 layers of cheesecloth. Discard solids. If using broth right away, skim off fat. *Or,* if storing broth for later use, chill in a bowl for 6 hours. Lift off fat. Pour broth into an airtight container; seal. Chill up to 3 days or freeze up to 3 months.

● When chicken is cool enough to handle, remove meat from bones. Discard skin and bones. Place meat in an airtight container; seal. Chill up to 3 days or freeze up to 1 month. Makes about 5 cups broth and about 4 cups meat.

For 1-quart crockery cooker: Not recommended.

Tex-Mex Chili

Tex-Mex Chili

Taste-panel-member Joyce predicted widespread popularity for this chili recipe.

1 pound ground beef *or* bulk
    pork sausage
2 cloves garlic, minced
3 to 4 teaspoons chili powder
½ teaspoon ground cumin
1 15½-ounce can red kidney
    beans, drained
1 cup chopped celery
1 cup chopped onion
½ cup chopped green pepper
1 16-ounce can tomatoes,
    cut up
1 10-ounce can tomatoes with
    green chili peppers
1 cup vegetable juice cocktail
    or tomato juice
1 6-ounce can tomato paste
¼ teaspoon salt
    Shredded cheddar cheese
    Dairy sour cream

● In a skillet cook beef or sausage and garlic till brown. Drain off fat. Stir in chili powder and cumin; cook 2 minutes more.

● Meanwhile, in a 3½-, 4-, 5-, or 6-quart crockery cooker combine beans, celery, onion, and green pepper. Add *undrained* tomatoes, *undrained* tomatoes with green chili peppers, vegetable juice cocktail or tomato juice, tomato paste, and salt. Stir in browned meat mixture.

● Cover; cook on low-heat setting for 10 to 12 hours or on high-heat setting for 4 to 5 hours.

● Ladle chili into soup bowls. Pass shredded cheese and sour cream with chili. Makes 4 to 6 servings.

For 1-quart crockery cooker: Halve ingredients. Prepare as above. *Do not* put kidney beans in the cooker. Heat kidney beans separately to pass with shredded cheddar cheese and sour cream. Cook chili 10 to 12 hours. Makes 2 or 3 servings.

Cider Stew

2 pounds beef stew meat
2 tablespoons cooking oil
3 medium potatoes, peeled
    and cubed (2½ cups)
3 medium carrots, cut into
    ½-inch pieces (1½ cups)
2 medium onions, sliced
1 medium apple, coarsely
    chopped (1 cup)
½ cup coarsely chopped celery
3 tablespoons quick-cooking
    tapioca
1 bay leaf
2 cups apple cider *or* apple
    juice
1 tablespoon vinegar
½ teaspoon salt
½ teaspoon caraway seed
¼ teaspoon dried thyme,
    crushed
¼ teaspoon pepper

● Cut meat into 1-inch cubes. In a large skillet brown meat, half at a time, in hot oil. Drain off fat.

● Meanwhile, in a 3½-, 4-, 5-, or 6-quart crockery cooker combine potatoes, carrots, onions, apple, celery, tapioca, and bay leaf. Stir in apple cider or juice, vinegar, salt, caraway seed, thyme, and pepper. Stir in browned meat.

● Cover; cook on low heat setting for 11 to 12 hours or high-heat setting for 5½ to 6 hours. Remove bay leaf. Serves 8.

For 1-quart crockery cooker: Use *½ pound* beef stew meat; *2 teaspoons* cooking oil; *1* potato, peeled and cubed; *1* carrot, cut into ½-inch pieces; *1 small* onion, sliced; *1 small* apple, coarsely chopped; *¼ cup* chopped celery; *2½ teaspoons* quick-cooking tapioca; *1* bay leaf; *½ cup* apple cider *or* apple juice; *1 teaspoon* vinegar; *⅛ teaspoon* salt; *⅛ teaspoon* caraway seed; *⅛ teaspoon* dried thyme, crushed; and *dash* pepper. Prepare as above. Cook for 10 to 12 hours. Makes 2 servings.

Old-Fashioned Vegetable-Beef Stew

1½ pounds beef stew meat
2 tablespoons cooking oil
2 medium potatoes, peeled and cubed (2 cups)
2 medium carrots, cut into ½-inch pieces (1 cup)
1 medium onion, cut into thin wedges
½ cup sliced celery
1 9-ounce package frozen cut green beans
3 tablespoons quick-cooking tapioca
1 tablespoon instant beef bouillon granules
2 teaspoons Worcestershire sauce
¾ teaspoon dried thyme, crushed
½ teaspoon salt
¼ teaspoon pepper
1 16-ounce can tomatoes, cut up
1½ cups water

● Cut meat into ½-inch cubes. In a large skillet brown meat, half at a time, in hot oil. Drain well.

● Meanwhile, in a 3½-, 4-, 5-, or 6-quart crockery cooker combine potatoes, carrots, onion, and celery. Add *frozen* beans, tapioca, bouillon granules, Worcestershire sauce, thyme, salt, and pepper. Stir in browned meat, *undrained* tomatoes, and water.

● Cover; cook on low-heat setting for 10 to 12 hours or high-heat setting for 5 to 6 hours. Makes 6 servings.

For 1-quart crockery cooker: Use ½ *pound* beef stew meat; *1 tablespoon* cooking oil; *1 medium* potato, peeled and cubed; *1 medium* carrot, cut into ½-inch pieces; *1 small* onion, cut into thin wedges; ¼ *cup* sliced celery; *1 cup* frozen cut green beans; *1 tablespoon* quick-cooking tapioca; *1 teaspoon* instant beef bouillon granules; ½ *teaspoon* Worcestershire sauce; ¼ *teaspoon* dried thyme, crushed; ¼ *teaspoon* salt; *dash* pepper; *one 7½-ounce can* tomatoes, cut up; and ½ *cup* water. Prepare as above. Cook for 10 to 12 hours. Makes 2 servings.

Beef-Barley Soup

A little spaghetti sauce rounds out the flavor of this homey soup.

1½ pounds beef stew meat
1 tablespoon cooking oil
1 cup thinly sliced carrots
1 cup sliced celery
1 medium onion, thinly sliced
½ cup coarsely chopped green pepper
¼ cup snipped parsley
4 cups beef broth
1 16-ounce can tomatoes, cut up
1 cup spaghetti sauce
⅔ cup pearl barley
1½ teaspoons dried basil, crushed
1 teaspoon salt
¼ teaspoon pepper

● Cut meat into 1-inch cubes. In a large skillet brown meat, half at a time, in hot oil. Drain well. Meanwhile, in a 3½-, 4-, 5-, or 6-quart crockery cooker combine carrots, celery, onion, green pepper, and parsley. Add broth, *undrained* tomatoes, spaghetti sauce, barley, basil, salt, and pepper. Stir in browned meat.

● Cover; cook on low-heat setting for 10 to 12 hours or on high-heat setting for 4½ to 5 hours. Skim off fat. Serves 6 to 8.

For 1-quart crockery cooker: Use ⅓ *pound* beef stew meat; *1 tablespoon* cooking oil; ⅓ *cup* sliced carrot *or* celery; *half of a small* onion, thinly sliced; *2 tablespoons* coarsely chopped green pepper; *1 tablespoon* snipped parsley; *1 cup* beef broth; *one 7½-ounce can* tomatoes, cut up; ¼ *cup* spaghetti sauce; *3 tablespoons* pearl barley; ½ *teaspoon* dried basil, crushed; ¼ *teaspoon* salt; and *dash* pepper. Prepare as above. Cook for 9 to 10 hours. Makes 2 servings.

Irish Stew

Generous servings for hearty appetites.

1 pound boneless lamb
2 tablespoons cooking oil
2 medium turnips, peeled and cut into ½-inch pieces (2½ cups)
3 medium carrots, cut into ½-inch pieces (1½ cups)
2 medium potatoes, peeled and cut into ½-inch pieces (1½ cups)
2 medium onions, cut into wedges
¼ cup quick-cooking tapioca
1 teaspoon salt
¼ teaspoon pepper
¼ teaspoon dried thyme, crushed
3 cups beef broth

● Cut lamb into 1-inch pieces. In a large skillet brown lamb, half at a time, in hot oil. Drain well.

● Meanwhile, in a 3½-, 4-, 5-, or 6-quart crockery cooker combine turnips, carrots, potatoes, onions, tapioca, salt, pepper, and thyme. Stir in browned lamb and beef broth.

● Cover; cook on low-heat setting for 10 to 12 hours or on high-heat setting for 5 to 6 hours. Makes 4 or 5 servings.

For 1-quart crockery cooker: Use *¼ pound* boneless lamb; *1 tablespoon* cooking oil; *1 small* turnip, peeled and cut into ½-inch pieces; *1 small* carrot, cut into ½-inch pieces; *1 small* potato, peeled and cut into ½-inch pieces; *1 small* onion, cut into wedges; *1 tablespoon* quick-cooking tapioca; *¼ teaspoon* salt; *dash* pepper; *pinch* dried thyme, crushed; and *¾ cup* beef broth. Prepare as above. Cook for 10 to 12 hours. Serves 1.

Hearty Sausage-Sauerkraut Soup

Sprinkle each bowl of soup with crumbled crisp-cooked bacon and chopped hard-cooked egg.

1½ cups chopped cooked chicken
8 ounces smoked Polish sausage links, chopped
1 small potato, cut into ½-inch pieces (¾ cup)
1 medium carrot, cut into ½-inch pieces (½ cup)
½ cup chopped onion
½ cup sliced celery
1 10¾-ounce can condensed cream of mushroom soup
1 8-ounce can sauerkraut, rinsed and drained
1 4-ounce can mushroom stems and pieces
1 tablespoon vinegar
1 teaspoon dried dillweed
¼ teaspoon pepper
2½ cups chicken broth

● In a 3½-, 4-, 5-, or 6-quart crockery cooker combine chicken, Polish sausage, potato, carrot, onion, and celery. Add mushroom soup, sauerkraut, *undrained* mushrooms, vinegar, dillweed, and pepper. Stir in chicken broth.

● Cover; cook on low-heat setting for 10 to 12 hours or on high-heat setting for 4½ to 5½ hours. Makes 4 servings.

For 1-quart crockery cooker: Use *½ cup* chopped cooked chicken; *3 ounces* smoked Polish sausage links, chopped; *⅓ cup chopped* potato; *¼ cup chopped* carrot; *¼ cup* chopped onion; *¼ cup* sliced celery; *½ cup* condensed cream of mushroom soup; *¼ cup* sauerkraut, rinsed and drained; *one 2-ounce can* mushroom stems and pieces (undrained); *1 teaspoon* vinegar; *½ teaspoon* dried dillweed; *dash* pepper; and *1¼ cups* chicken broth. Prepare as above. Cook for 10 to 12 hours. Makes 2 servings.

Pork Stew with
Cornmeal Dumplings

Pork Stew with Cornmeal Dumplings

If you don't have time to make dumplings, follow our advice in the directions for the 1-quart cooker: skip the dumplings and serve corn muffins with the stew. (Pictured on the cover.)

1 1-pound boneless pork
   shoulder roast
1 clove garlic, minced
1 tablespoon cooking oil
4 medium carrots, cut into
   ½-inch pieces (2 cups)
2 medium potatoes, peeled
   and cubed (2 cups)
1 12-ounce can (1½ cups) beer
¼ cup quick-cooking tapioca
1 tablespoon sugar
1 tablespoon Worcestershire
   sauce
2 bay leaves
1 teaspoon dried thyme,
   crushed
½ teaspoon salt
¼ teaspoon ground nutmeg
¼ teaspoon pepper
1 28-ounce can tomatoes,
   cut up
   Cornmeal Dumplings (see
   recipe, below)
2 tablespoons shredded
   cheddar cheese

● Cut pork into 1-inch cubes. In a large skillet brown pork and garlic in hot oil. Drain well.

● Meanwhile, in a 3½- or 4-quart crockery cooker combine carrots, potatoes, beer, tapioca, sugar, Worcestershire sauce, bay leaves, thyme, salt, nutmeg, and pepper. Stir in browned meat and *undrained* tomatoes. Cover; cook on low-heat setting for 9 to 11 hours or on high-heat setting for 4 to 5 hours.

● If stew was cooked on low-heat setting, turn crockery cooker to high-heat setting. Prepare Cornmeal Dumplings. Remove bay leaves. Stir stew; drop dumplings by tablespoonfuls onto stew. Cover; cook for 50 minutes more (*do not lift cover*). Sprinkle dumplings with cheese. Makes 4 servings.

For 5- or 6-quart crockery cooker: Use *one 1½-pound* boneless pork shoulder roast, *5 medium* carrots, and *3 medium* potatoes. Leave remaining ingredient amounts the same. Prepare as above. Makes 6 servings.

For 1-quart crockery cooker: Use *1 medium* carrot, halve remaining stew ingredients, and omit Cornmeal Dumplings and cheese. Prepare as above. Cook for 10 to 12 hours. Serve stew with corn muffins or corn bread. Makes 2 servings.

Cornmeal Dumplings

½ cup all-purpose flour
½ cup shredded cheddar
   cheese
⅓ cup yellow cornmeal
1 teaspoon baking powder
   Dash pepper
1 beaten egg
2 tablespoons milk
2 tablespoons cooking oil

● In a medium mixing bowl stir together flour, cheddar cheese, cornmeal, baking powder, and pepper.

● Combine beaten egg, milk, and oil. Add to flour mixture; stir with a fork just till combined. Use in Pork Stew with Cornmeal Dumplings, above.

Chicken and
Sausage Gumbo

Chicken and Sausage Gumbo

The toasty flavor of the roux (roo) is well worth the extra effort.

⅓ cup all-purpose flour
⅓ cup cooking oil
3 cups water
12 ounces fully cooked smoked sausage links, sliced and quartered
2 cups chopped cooked chicken
2 cups sliced okra *or* one 10-ounce package frozen whole okra, sliced ½ inch thick
1 cup chopped onion
½ cup chopped green pepper
½ cup chopped celery
4 cloves garlic, minced
1 teaspoon salt
½ teaspoon pepper
¼ teaspoon ground red pepper
Hot cooked rice

● For roux, in a heavy 2-quart saucepan stir together flour and oil till smooth. Cook over medium-high heat 5 minutes, stirring constantly. Reduce heat to medium. Cook and stir constantly about 15 minutes more or till a dark, reddish brown roux forms. Cool.

● In a 3½-, 4-, 5-, or 6-quart crockery cooker place water. Stir in roux. Add sausage, chicken, okra, onion, green pepper, celery, garlic, salt, pepper, and red pepper. Cover; cook on low-heat setting for 10 to 12 hours or on high-heat setting for 4½ to 5 hours. Skim off fat. Serve over rice. Makes 6 servings.

For 1-quart crockery cooker: Use *2 tablespoons* all-purpose flour; *2 tablespoons* cooking oil; *1 cup* water; *4 ounces* fully cooked smoked sausage links, sliced and quartered; *⅔ cup* chopped cooked chicken; *⅔ cup* sliced okra; *⅓ cup* chopped onion; *2 tablespoons* chopped green pepper; *2 tablespoons* chopped celery; *1 clove* garlic, minced; *½ teaspoon* salt; *⅛ teaspoon* pepper; *⅛ teaspoon* ground red pepper; and hot cooked rice. Prepare as above. Cook for 10 to 12 hours. Serves 2.

Making a roux

A *heavy* saucepan and a long-handled wooden spoon will make it easier to cook and stir your roux.

When the roux matches the reddish brown color of a tarnished copper penny, remove it from the heat. Because the mixture is extremely hot, let it cool before combining it with the other ingredients.

Since making roux is a lengthy process, consider doubling the ingredients and storing half of the mixture for a future gumbo.

Cover the roux and refrigerate it up to 2 weeks or freeze it up to 6 months.

Ham-and-Bean Vegetable Soup

3 cups water
½ pound dry navy beans
    (1¼ cups)
1 medium potato, peeled and
    cut into ½-inch pieces
    (1 cup)
1 medium carrot, cut into
    ½-inch pieces (½ cup)
1 stalk celery, sliced (½ cup)
½ cup chopped onion
2 tablespoons snipped parsley
½ teaspoon dried thyme,
    crushed
¼ teaspoon salt
⅛ teaspoon pepper
    Dash bottled hot pepper
    sauce
4 cups water
¾ pound meaty smoked pork
    hocks

● In a 3-quart saucepan bring 3 cups water and beans to boiling. Boil, uncovered, for 10 minutes. Drain.

● Meanwhile, in a 3½- or 4-quart crockery cooker combine potato, carrot, celery, onion, parsley, thyme, salt, pepper, and hot pepper sauce. Stir in drained beans and 4 cups water. Place pork hocks atop bean mixture.

● Cover; cook on low-heat setting for 10 to 12 hours or on high-heat setting for 4½ to 5½ hours.

● Lift pork hocks from soup. Remove meat from bones; chop meat and return to soup. Discard bones. Makes 5 servings.

For 5- or 6-quart crockery cooker: Double all ingredients. Prepare as above. Makes 10 servings.

For 1-quart crockery cooker: Not recommended.

Cutting vegetables to size
Vegetables intended for the crockery cooker are cut into bite-size pieces not only for convenience in eating, but for better cooking, too.

    Surprisingly, vegetables can take longer to cook than meat in crockery cookers. By cutting the vegetables into smaller pieces (about ½ inch), you can be sure they will be tender when the meat is done.

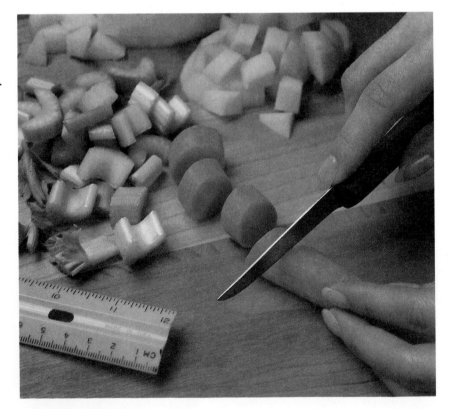

South American Pork Soup

Sophisticated and tasty.

1 pound boneless pork *or* beef stew meat
1 tablespoon cooking oil
½ cup chopped onion
2 cloves garlic, minced
1 teaspoon paprika
3 cups water
2 medium parsnips *or* 3 medium carrots, cut into ¼-inch pieces (1½ cups)
½ pound winter squash, peeled and cut into ½-inch pieces (1½ cups)
1 medium sweet potato, peeled and cut into ½-inch pieces (1⅓ cups)
1 8-ounce can whole kernel corn
4 teaspoons instant beef bouillon granules
1 teaspoon salt
¼ teaspoon ground red pepper
2 cups torn fresh spinach

● Cut meat into ½-inch cubes. In a large skillet brown *half* of the meat in hot oil. Remove meat; set aside. Brown remaining meat with onion, garlic, and paprika.

● Meanwhile, in a 3½-, 4-, 5-, or 6-quart crockery cooker place water, parsnips or carrots, squash, sweet potato, *undrained* corn, beef bouillon granules, salt, and red pepper. Stir in browned meat and browned meat-onion mixture.

● Cover; cook on low-heat setting for 10 to 12 hours or on high-heat setting for 5 to 6 hours.

● Before serving, add torn spinach to soup and stir till slightly wilted. Makes 4 servings.

For 1-quart crockery cooker: Use *6 ounces* boneless pork *or* beef stew meat; *1 tablespoon* cooking oil; *¼ cup* chopped onion; *1 clove* garlic, minced; *½ teaspoon* paprika; *1¼ cups* water; *1½ cups cubed* parsnip, carrot, winter squash, *or* sweet potato; *⅓ cup* whole kernel corn; *2 teaspoons* instant beef bouillon granules; *¼ teaspoon* salt; *⅛ teaspoon* ground red pepper; and *¾ cup* torn fresh spinach. Prepare as above. Cook for 10 to 12 hours. Makes 2 servings.

Sweet Potato and Sausage Stew

Smoked turkey sausage has all the flavor of traditional pork sausage but fewer calories.

1 pound smoked turkey sausage link
2 small sweet potatoes, peeled and cut into ½-inch pieces (2 cups)
1 medium green pepper, cut into 1-inch pieces (¾ cup)
1 stalk celery, cut into ½-inch pieces (½ cup)
½ cup chopped onion
2 tablespoons quick-cooking tapioca
1 16-ounce can tomatoes, cut up
1 15-ounce can garbanzo beans, drained
1 cup beef broth

● Cut sausage in half lengthwise; cut into 1-inch-thick slices. In a 3½-, 4-, 5-, or 6-quart crockery cooker combine sausage pieces, sweet potatoes, green pepper, celery, onion, and tapioca. Add *undrained* tomatoes, garbanzo beans, and beef broth.

● Cover; cook on low-heat setting for 10 to 12 hours or on high-heat setting for 4½ to 5 hours. Makes 4 servings.

For 1-quart crockery cooker: Not recommended.

Brunswick Stew

Brunswick Stew

Keep the menu simple. Serve sliced French or Vienna bread with the hearty stew and scoops of ice cream for dessert.

1 16-ounce can tomatoes, cut up
1 6-ounce can tomato paste
3 cups chopped cooked chicken
1 10-ounce package frozen succotash *or* one 10-ounce package frozen whole okra, sliced ½ inch thick
1 cup chopped onion
1 bay leaf
1 teaspoon salt
½ teaspoon dried rosemary, crushed
½ teaspoon pepper
Dash ground cloves
2½ cups chicken broth

● In a 3½-, 4-, 5-, or 6-quart crockery cooker stir together *undrained* tomatoes and tomato paste. Add chicken, frozen succotash or sliced okra, onion, bay leaf, salt, rosemary, pepper, and cloves. Stir in chicken broth.

● Cover; cook on low-heat setting for 10 to 12 hours or on high-heat setting for 5 to 6 hours. Before serving, remove bay leaf and stir well. Makes 6 servings.

For 1-quart crockery cooker: Not recommended.

Chicken-Linguine Soup

Set the pea pods out to thaw when you add the linguine to the soup, then relax the final hour before dinner.

2½ cups chopped cooked chicken
2 medium carrots, bias-sliced ¼ inch thick
2 tablespoons dry sherry
2 tablespoons soy sauce
½ teaspoon grated gingerroot *or* ¼ teaspoon ground ginger
¼ teaspoon pepper
6 cups chicken broth
2 ounces linguine, broken into pieces
1 6-ounce package frozen pea pods, thawed

● In a 3½-, 4-, 5-, or 6-quart crockery cooker combine chicken, carrots, sherry, soy sauce, gingerroot or ground ginger, and pepper. Stir in chicken broth. Cover; cook on low-heat setting for 9 to 11 hours or on high-heat setting for 4 to 5 hours.

● Stir in linguine. Cover; cook on low-heat or high-heat setting for 1 hour more. Before serving, stir in *thawed* pea pods. Makes 6 servings.

For 1-quart crockery cooker: Use ¾ *cup* chopped cooked chicken; *1 small* carrot, bias-sliced ¼ inch thick; *1 tablespoon* dry sherry; *1 tablespoon* soy sauce; *dash* ground ginger; *dash* pepper; and *2 cups* chicken broth. Prepare as above. Cook for 9 to 11 hours. Stir in ¾ *ounce* linguine, broken into pieces. Cover and cook 1 hour more. Before serving, stir in ¾ *cup* frozen pea pods, thawed. Makes 2 servings.

Oriental Hot-and-Sour Soup

Oriental Hot-and-Sour Soup

4 cups chicken broth
1 8-ounce can bamboo shoots, drained
1 8-ounce can sliced water chestnuts, drained
1 6-ounce can sliced mushrooms, drained
3 tablespoons quick-cooking tapioca
3 tablespoons rice wine vinegar *or* vinegar
1 tablespoon soy sauce
1 teaspoon sugar
½ teaspoon pepper
1 8-ounce package frozen peeled and deveined shrimp
4 ounces tofu (fresh bean curd), cubed
1 beaten egg
2 tablespoons snipped parsley *or* fresh coriander

● In a 3½- or 4-quart crockery cooker combine broth, bamboo shoots, water chestnuts, mushrooms, tapioca, vinegar, soy sauce, sugar, and pepper. Cover; cook on low-heat setting for 9 to 11 hours or on high-heat setting for 3 to 4 hours. Add shrimp and tofu. Cover; cook on low- or high-heat setting for 50 minutes more. Pour egg slowly into cooker; stir till egg cooks and shreds. Top with parsley. Makes 8 appetizer servings.

For 5- to 6-quart crockery cooker: Use *5 cups* chicken broth, *¼ cup* quick-cooking tapioca, *¼ cup* rice wine vinegar, and *2 tablespoons* soy sauce. Leave remaining ingredient amounts the same. Prepare as above. Makes 9 appetizer servings.

For 1-quart crockery cooker: Use *1⅓ cups* chicken broth; *½ cup* drained bamboo shoots; *½ cup* sliced water chestnuts; *one 2½-ounce can* sliced mushrooms, drained; *1 tablespoon* quick-cooking tapioca; *1 tablespoon* rice wine vinegar; *1 teaspoon* soy sauce; *¼ teaspoon* sugar; and *¼ teaspoon* pepper. Prepare as above. Cook for 9 to 11 hours. Add *3 ounces* frozen peeled and deveined shrimp and *1 ounce* cubed tofu. Cook for 50 minutes more. Stir in *2 tablespoons* beaten egg till egg cooks and shreds. Top with *1 tablespoon* snipped parsley *or* coriander. Serves 3.

Adding the egg
Pour the beaten egg slowly into the soup in a thin stream. Stir the soup gently so that the egg forms fine shreds instead of clumps.

Fish Stew

Don't worry about completely thawing the fish. It goes into the cooker partially frozen.

1 16-ounce package frozen haddock *or* sole fillets
2 medium potatoes, peeled and finely chopped
2 medium carrots, finely chopped
¼ cup snipped parsley
1 bay leaf
1 tablespoon quick-cooking tapioca
1 teaspoon sugar
¼ teaspoon salt
¼ teaspoon dried basil, crushed
1 16-ounce can tomatoes, cut up
1 14½-ounce can chicken broth
1 8-ounce can tomato sauce
¼ cup dry sherry *or* water

● Let fish stand at room temperature while preparing other ingredients. In a 3½-, 4-, 5-, or 6-quart crockery cooker combine potatoes, carrots, parsley, bay leaf, tapioca, sugar, salt, basil, and ⅛ teaspoon *pepper*. Stir in *undrained* tomatoes, chicken broth, tomato sauce, and sherry or water.

● Halve block of fish crosswise; place halves in the cooker. Cover; cook on low-heat setting for 10 to 12 hours or on high-heat setting for 3½ to 4 hours. Remove bay leaf. Break fish into bite-size chunks with a fork. Makes 4 servings.

For 1-quart crockery cooker: Omit tomato sauce. Use *2 individually frozen* fish fillets; *1 small* potato, peeled and finely chopped; *1 small* carrot, finely chopped; *1 tablespoon* snipped parsley; *1 small* bay leaf; *2 teaspoons* quick-cooking tapioca; ¼ *teaspoon* sugar; ⅛ *teaspoon* salt; ⅛ *teaspoon* dried basil, crushed; *dash pepper; one 7½-ounce can* tomatoes, cut up; ½ *cup* chicken broth; and *1 tablespoon* dry sherry *or* water. Prepare as above. Cook for 9 to 10 hours. Makes 2 servings.

Cheesy Salmon Chowder

Cheese lovers, take note!

2 medium carrots, sliced ¼ inch thick
1 cup chopped celery
½ cup chopped onion
½ cup wheat berries
2 14½-ounce cans chicken broth
1 cup water
1 8-ounce package cream cheese, cut into cubes
1 cup shredded process Swiss cheese (4 ounces)
1 cup frozen peas
1 15½-ounce can salmon, drained, flaked, and skin and bones removed

● In a 3½- or 4-quart crockery cooker combine carrots, celery, onion, and wheat berries. Stir in chicken broth and water. Cover; cook on low-heat setting for 10 to 11 hours or on high-heat setting for 4 to 4½ hours.

● If cooker was on low-heat setting, turn to high-heat setting. Add cream cheese, Swiss cheese, and peas. Cover; cook for 30 to 60 minutes more or till cheeses are melted. Just before serving, stir in salmon. Makes 6 servings.

For 5- or 6-quart crockery cooker: Not recommended.

For 1-quart crockery cooker: Omit water. Use *1 small* carrot, sliced ¼ inch thick; ⅓ *cup* chopped celery; ¼ *cup* chopped onion; *3 tablespoons* wheat berries; and *one 14½-ounce can* chicken broth. Prepare as above. Cook for 9 to 10 hours. Add *one 3-ounce package* cream cheese, cubed; ½ *cup* shredded process Swiss cheese; and ⅓ *cup* frozen peas. Cook 1 hour more. Just before serving, stir in *one 7¾-ounce can* salmon, drained, flaked, and skin and bones removed. Serves 2.

Clam Chowder

The bacon or salt pork lends smokiness to this rich soup.

3 slices bacon, cut up, *or*
    ¼ pound salt pork, diced
2 6½-ounce cans minced
    clams
3 medium potatoes, peeled
    and cut into bite-size
    pieces (3 cups)
1 cup chopped onion
1 medium carrot, shredded
1 10¾-ounce can condensed
    cream of mushroom soup
¼ teaspoon pepper
2 12-ounce cans (3 cups)
    evaporated milk

● In a skillet cook bacon or salt pork till crisp; drain. Drain clams, reserving liquid; add water to liquid to equal 1¾ cups. Cover clams; chill.

● In a 3½- or 4-quart crockery cooker combine reserved clam liquid, potatoes, onion, and carrot. Stir in mushroom soup and pepper. Add bacon or salt pork. Cover; cook on low-heat setting for 9 to 11 hours or on high-heat setting for 4 to 5 hours.

● If cooker was on low-heat setting, turn to high-heat setting. Stir in clams and evaporated milk. Cover; cook for 1 hour more. Makes 6 servings.

For 5- or 6-quart crockery cooker: Use *6 slices* bacon, cut up, or *6 ounces* salt pork, diced; *three 6½-ounce cans* minced clams; *2½ cups* reserved clam liquid; *3 large* potatoes, peeled and cut into bite-size pieces; *1½ cups* chopped onion; *1 large* carrot, shredded; *two 10¾-ounce cans* condensed cream of mushroom soup; *¼ teaspoon* pepper; and *three 12-ounce cans* evaporated milk. Prepare as above. Makes 9 servings.

For 1-quart crockery cooker: Use *2 slices* bacon, cut up, or *2 ounces* salt pork, diced; *one 6½-ounce can* minced clams; *¾ cup* reserved clam liquid; *2 medium* potatoes, peeled and cut into bite-size pieces; *½ cup* chopped onion; *1 small* carrot, shredded; *half of a 10¾-ounce can (⅔ cup)* condensed cream of mushroom soup; and *⅛ teaspoon* pepper. Prepare as above. Cook for 9 to 11 hours. Stir in reserved clams and *1 cup* evaporated milk. Cook 1 hour more. Makes 3 servings.

Breads to Accompany Soups and Stews

Freshly baked bread is the ideal complement to a crockery dinner of soup or stew. But who has the time to make bread? This section provides a few answers.

In the time it takes to preheat your oven, for example, you can mix the muffins, below, or the popovers and drop biscuits, opposite. For make-ahead ease, try the yeast breads on pages 56 and 57. Just leave the dough in the refrigerator to rise overnight, then pop it into the oven right before it's time to serve dinner.

Mammoth Muffins

Giant muffins for big appetites. (Pictured on pages 54–55.)

1½ cups all-purpose flour
½ cup quick-cooking rolled oats
2½ teaspoons baking powder
¼ teaspoon salt
2 beaten eggs
¾ cup milk
⅓ cup packed brown sugar
⅓ cup cooking oil
½ cup bran flakes

● In a large mixing bowl stir together flour, quick-cooking rolled oats, baking powder, and salt. In another bowl combine eggs, milk, sugar, and cooking oil; stir in bran flakes. Add to flour mixture. Stir just till moistened (batter will be thick).

● Divide batter equally among 4 greased 6-ounce custard cups. Set cups 2 inches apart in a shallow baking pan. Bake in a 375° oven for 30 to 35 minutes or till a wooden toothpick inserted near the centers comes out clean. Cool 5 minutes in cups. Remove muffins from cups and serve warm. Makes 4 muffins.

Easy Italian Spirals

Great with the Beef-Barley Soup recipe on page 38. (Spirals pictured on pages 54–55.)

2 cups whole wheat flour
2 tablespoons grated Parmesan cheese
2 teaspoons baking powder
¼ teaspoon dried basil, crushed
¼ teaspoon dried oregano, crushed
⅛ teaspoon garlic salt
½ cup margarine *or* butter
1 beaten egg
½ cup milk
½ cup shredded mozzarella cheese (2 ounces)
Melted margarine *or* butter, *or* milk
Poppy seed

● In a large mixing bowl stir together flour, Parmesan cheese, baking powder, basil, oregano, and garlic salt. Cut in ½ cup margarine or butter till mixture resembles coarse crumbs. Make a well in the center. Combine egg and ½ cup milk; add all at once to dry ingredients. Stir just till dough clings together.

● Knead dough gently on a lightly floured surface for 12 to 15 strokes. Roll dough into a 15x8-inch rectangle. Sprinkle mozzarella cheese over dough. Fold dough in half lengthwise to make a 15x4-inch rectangle. Cut into fifteen 4x1-inch strips.

● Holding a strip at both ends, twist twice in opposite directions to form a spiral. Place twisted strip on a lightly greased baking sheet, pressing both ends down. Repeat with remaining strips. Brush strips with melted margarine or butter or with milk. Sprinkle with poppy seed. Bake in a 450° oven for 8 to 10 minutes or till golden. Serve warm. Makes 15.

Onion 'n' Cheese Popovers

Popovers sound so special, yet they're not hard to make.

1½ teaspoons shortening
2 beaten eggs
1 cup milk
1 tablespoon cooking oil
1 cup all-purpose flour
2 tablespoons grated
   Parmesan cheese
1 teaspoon dried parsley
   flakes *or* snipped dried
   chives
¼ teaspoon onion powder
⅛ teaspoon salt

● Using *¼ teaspoon* shortening for *each* cup, grease the bottoms and sides of six 6-ounce custard cups or the cups of a 6-unit popover pan. Place the custard cups in a shallow baking pan; set aside. *Or,* set popover pan in the oven while it preheats.

● In a medium mixing bowl combine eggs, milk, and oil. Add flour, Parmesan cheese, dried parsley or chives, onion powder, and salt. Beat with a rotary beater till smooth. (*Or,* in a blender container combine *unbeaten* eggs, milk, and oil; blend till smooth. Add flour, Parmesan cheese, parsley or chives, onion powder, and salt; blend till smooth.)

● Fill custard cups or hot popover cups *half* full. Bake in a 450° oven for 20 minutes. Reduce heat to 350°; bake about 20 minutes more or till very firm. (If popovers brown too quickly, turn off oven and finish baking them in the cooling oven.) A few minutes before removing popovers from oven, prick each with a fork to let steam escape. If desired, for crisper popovers, remove popovers from cups and place on their sides in the baking or popover pan. Bake 5 to 7 minutes more. Serve hot. Makes 6.

● **Pumpernickel Popovers:** Prepare and bake as above, *except* omit Parmesan cheese, use only ⅔ cup all-purpose flour, and increase salt to ¼ *teaspoon.* Add ⅓ cup *rye flour* and 1 teaspoon *caraway seed* to dry ingredients.

● **Orange-Nut Popovers:** Prepare and bake as above, *except* omit Parmesan cheese, parsley or chives, and onion powder. Stir ¼ cup finely chopped *pecans* and ¼ teaspoon finely shredded *orange peel* into batter.

Caraway-Rye Drop Biscuits

Try these quick biscuits with the Ham-and-Bean Vegetable Soup recipe on page 44.

1½ cups all-purpose flour
½ cup rye flour
1 tablespoon baking powder
1 teaspoon sugar
1 teaspoon caraway seed
½ teaspoon cream of tartar
¼ teaspoon salt
½ cup shortening
1 cup milk

● In a medium mixing bowl stir together all-purpose flour, rye flour, baking powder, sugar, caraway seed, cream of tartar, and salt. Cut in shortening till mixture resembles coarse crumbs.

● Make a well in the center. Add milk all at once. Stir just till dough clings together.

● Drop dough from a tablespoon onto a greased baking sheet. Bake in a 450° oven for 10 to 12 minutes or till golden. Serve warm. Makes 12 biscuits.

Easy Italian Spirals
(see recipe, page 52)

Pull-Apart Loaves
(see recipe, page 56)

Ham and Cheese Bread
(see recipe, page 56)

Mammoth Muffins
(see recipe, page 52)

Ham and Cheese Bread

Use a sharp knife to cut the X on the bread. (Pictured on page 55.)

2 tablespoons grated
 Parmesan cheese
2½ to 3 cups all-purpose flour
1 package active dry yeast
¾ cup milk
1 tablespoon sugar
¼ teaspoon salt
½ cup shredded cheddar
 cheese (2 ounces)
1 egg
¾ cup finely chopped fully
 cooked ham
1 tablespoon Parmesan
 cheese

● Generously grease a 1½-quart soufflé dish; coat with 2 tablespoons Parmesan cheese. In a large mixer bowl combine *1 cup* flour and yeast. Heat milk, sugar, and salt just till warm (120° to 130°), stirring constantly. Add to flour mixture. Add cheddar cheese and egg. Beat with an electric mixer on low speed for 30 seconds, scraping bowl. Beat on high speed for 3 minutes.

● Using a spoon, stir in ham and as much remaining flour as you can. On a lightly floured surface knead in enough remaining flour to make a moderately stiff dough (6 to 8 minutes total). Shape dough into a ball. Place in prepared dish. Press to flatten. Sprinkle top with 1 tablespoon Parmesan cheese; cut an X about ½ inch deep on the top. Cover loosely with clear plastic wrap. Refrigerate 2 to 24 hours.

● **To serve:** Remove cover; let bread stand at room temperature for 20 minutes. Puncture air bubbles using a greased wooden toothpick. Bake in a 350° oven for 40 to 45 minutes or till golden. Cover with foil the last 15 minutes to prevent overbrowning. Remove from dish. Cool on a wire rack. Makes 1 loaf.

Pull-Apart Loaves

Mix and match the toppings to suit your taste. (Pictured on page 54.)

5¾ to 6¼ cups all-purpose flour
1 package active dry yeast
2¼ cups milk
2 tablespoons sugar
1 tablespoon shortening
1 teaspoon salt
 Melted margarine *or* butter
 Assorted toppings: sesame
  seed, poppy seed, caraway
  seed, dillweed, toasted
  wheat germ, cornmeal,
  grated Parmesan cheese,
  or rolled oats

● In a large mixer bowl combine *2½ cups* flour and yeast. Heat milk, sugar, shortening, and salt just till warm (120° to 130°), stirring constantly. Add to flour mixture. Beat with an electric mixer on low speed for 30 seconds, scraping bowl. Beat on high speed for 3 minutes. Using a spoon, stir in as much of the remaining flour as you can. On a lightly floured surface knead in enough of the remaining flour to make a moderately stiff dough that is smooth and elastic (6 to 8 minutes total). Cover; let rest 10 minutes.

● Divide dough into 16 pieces; shape into balls. Place 8 balls in *each* of 2 greased 8x4x2-inch loaf pans. Brush with melted margarine. Sprinkle each ball with a different topping. Cover loosely with clear plastic wrap. Refrigerate 2 to 24 hours.

● **To serve:** Let loaves stand, uncovered, at room temperature for 10 minutes. Puncture air bubbles with a greased wooden toothpick. Bake in a 375° oven for 40 to 45 minutes or till golden. Cover with foil the last 10 minutes to prevent overbrowning. Remove from pans; cool. Makes 2 loaves.

Whole Wheat Freezer Breadsticks

Make the breadsticks ahead and freeze. Then bake a few at a time as needed.

1 to 1½ cups all-purpose flour
2 packages active dry yeast
¾ cup milk
2 tablespoons shortening
1 tablespoon sugar
½ teaspoon salt
½ cup whole wheat flour
1 egg white
1 tablespoon water
   Sesame seed

● In a small mixer bowl stir together ¾ *cup* all-purpose flour and yeast. In a saucepan heat milk, shortening, sugar, and salt just till warm (120° to 130°), stirring constantly. Add to flour mixture. Beat with an electric mixer on low speed for 30 seconds, scraping sides of bowl constantly. Beat on high speed for 3 minutes. Using a spoon, stir in whole wheat flour and as much of the remaining all-purpose flour as you can.

● On a lightly floured surface knead in enough remaining all-purpose flour to make a stiff dough that is smooth and elastic (8 to 10 minutes total). Cover and let rest 10 minutes.

● Divide dough into 24 pieces. Roll each piece into a rope 8 inches long. Place on a greased baking sheet. Cover with clear plastic wrap and freeze till firm. Transfer breadsticks to a freezer bag; seal and label. Store in the freezer up to 4 weeks.

● **To serve:** Remove breadsticks from freezer; place on a greased baking sheet. Cover loosely with clear plastic wrap. Let thaw and rise at room temperature for 1 hour. (*Or,* thaw in refrigerator for 8 to 24 hours. Remove from refrigerator; let rise in a warm place for 15 to 20 minutes.)

● In a small bowl mix egg white and water. Brush breadsticks with egg-white mixture. Sprinkle with sesame seed. Bake in a 375° oven for 10 to 12 minutes or till golden. If desired, for a hard breadstick, reduce oven temperature to 300° and bake for 15 to 20 minutes more. Makes 24 breadsticks.

Onion Rolls

The onion flavor blends well with the Lentil-Mushroom Soup recipe on page 59.

2½ cups all-purpose flour
3 tablespoons *regular* onion
   soup mix
1 package active dry yeast
1 cup warm water (120° to
   130°)
2 tablespoons sugar
2 tablespoons cooking oil
1 egg

● In a large mixer bowl combine *1½ cups* flour, dry onion soup mix, and yeast. In a small mixing bowl combine water, sugar, and oil. Add water mixture to flour mixture; add egg. Beat with an electric mixer on low speed for 30 seconds, scraping sides of bowl constantly. Beat on high speed for 3 minutes. Using a spoon, stir in remaining flour. Cover and let rise in a warm place till double (about 30 minutes).

● Spoon batter into 12 greased muffin cups. Cover and let rise till nearly double (about 25 minutes). Bake in a 375° oven for 15 to 18 minutes or till lightly browned. Remove rolls from pan. Cool on a wire rack. Makes 12 rolls.

Chunky Chowder

Chunks of potatoes, fish, and vegetables make this a hearty soup.

1 pound fresh *or* frozen sole
   or haddock fillets
5 slices bacon, cut up
2 medium potatoes, peeled
   and chopped (2 cups)
½ cup chopped onion
½ cup chopped celery
2 tablespoons snipped parsley
1 10-ounce package frozen
   mixed vegetables
1 8¾-ounce can cream-style
   corn
1 cup water
1 teaspoon dried dillweed
¼ teaspoon celery seed
1 12-ounce can (1½ cups)
   evaporated milk

● Thaw fish, if frozen. Cut into 1½-inch pieces and set aside. In a skillet cook bacon till crisp; drain.

● Meanwhile, in a 3½-, 4-, 5-, or 6-quart crockery cooker combine potatoes, onion, celery, and parsley. Add frozen vegetables, cream-style corn, water, dillweed, and celery seed. Stir in fish and bacon. Cover; cook on low-heat setting for 9 to 11 hours or on high-heat setting for 3½ to 4½ hours.

● Stir in evaporated milk. Cover; cook on low-heat or high-heat setting for 1 hour more. Season to taste with salt and pepper. Makes 4 servings.

For 1-quart crockery cooker: Omit cream-style corn and halve remaining ingredients. Prepare as above. Cook for 9 to 11 hours. Stir in evaporated milk. Cook 1 hour more. Season to taste with salt and pepper. Makes 2 servings.

Five-Bean Soup

An easy soup with a south-of-the-border flavor.

1 15½-ounce can red kidney
   beans
1 15-ounce can garbanzo
   beans
1 15-ounce can navy beans
1 8½-ounce can lima beans
1 9-ounce package frozen cut
   green beans
1 cup chopped onion
1 4-ounce can diced green
   chili peppers, drained
4 teaspoons chili powder
1½ teaspoons dried basil,
   crushed
½ teaspoon dried oregano,
   crushed
¼ teaspoon bottled hot pepper
   sauce
2½ cups beef broth
1 12-ounce can beer
1 cup shredded cheddar
   cheese (4 ounces)

● Drain kidney beans, garbanzo beans, navy beans, and lima beans. In a 3½-, 4-, 5-, or 6-quart crockery cooker combine drained beans, frozen green beans, chopped onion, chili peppers, chili powder, basil, oregano, and hot pepper sauce. Stir in beef broth and beer.

● Cover; cook on low-heat setting for 10 to 12 hours or on high-heat setting for 5 to 6 hours. Ladle into soup bowls. Top each serving with shredded cheese. Makes 8 servings.

For 1-quart crockery cooker: Not recommended.

Lentil-Mushroom Soup

A dollop of sour cream heightens the flavors of this main-dish soup.

½ pound dry lentils (1¼ cups)
2 medium carrots, sliced
   ¼ inch thick
1 medium onion, chopped
1 cup sliced celery
¼ cup snipped parsley
3 cups water
1 10¾-ounce can condensed
   cream of mushroom soup
2 teaspoons instant beef
   bouillon granules
Dairy sour cream

● In a 3½- or 4-quart crockery cooker combine lentils, carrots, onion, celery, and parsley. Stir in water, mushroom soup, and bouillon granules. Cover; cook on low-heat setting for 10 to 12 hours or on high-heat setting for 5 to 6 hours. Top each serving with a dollop of sour cream. Makes 4 servings.

For 5- or 6-quart crockery cooker: Use *8 cups* water and *2 tablespoons* instant beef bouillon granules. Double remaining ingredients. Prepare as above. Makes 8 servings.

For 1-quart crockery cooker: Not recommended.

French Onion Soup

Fit this appetizer into your schedule by cooking it as little as 2½ hours or up to 10 hours.

4 to 6 onions, thinly sliced
   (4 to 6 cups)
1 clove garlic, minced
3 tablespoons margarine
   or butter
3 10½-ounce cans condensed
   beef broth
1 cup water
1½ teaspoons Worcestershire
   sauce
⅛ teaspoon pepper
6 to 8 1-inch slices French
   bread
6 to 8 ¾-ounce slices Swiss
   or Gruyère cheese

● In a large skillet cook onions and garlic in hot margarine or butter, covered, over medium-low heat about 20 minutes or till tender, stirring occasionally.

● Transfer onion mixture to a 3½- or 4-quart crockery cooker. Add condensed beef broth, water, Worcestershire sauce, and pepper. Cover; cook on low-heat setting for 5 to 10 hours or on high-heat setting for 2½ to 3 hours.

● Before serving soup, toast bread slices. Then arrange toast slices on a baking sheet and top *each* with a slice of cheese; broil 3 to 4 inches from the heat for 3 to 4 minutes or till cheese is light brown and bubbly. Ladle soup into bowls; top with toast. Makes 6 to 8 appetizer servings.

For 5- or 6-quart crockery cooker: Use *6 to 8* onions, thinly sliced; *1 clove* garlic, minced; *¼ cup* margarine or butter; *four 10½-ounce cans* condensed beef broth; *1½ cups* water; *2 teaspoons* Worcestershire sauce; *⅛ teaspoon* pepper; *10 to 12 slices* French bread; and *10 to 12 slices* Swiss or Gruyère cheese. Prepare as above. Makes 10 to 12 appetizer servings.

For 1-quart crockery cooker: Use *2* onions, thinly sliced; *1 small clove* garlic, minced; *1 tablespoon* margarine or butter; *one 10½-ounce can* condensed beef broth; *⅓ cup* water; *½ teaspoon* Worcestershire sauce; *dash* pepper; *2 or 3 slices* French bread; and *2 or 3 slices* Swiss or Gruyère cheese. Prepare as above. Cook for 5 to 10 hours. Makes 2 or 3 appetizer servings.

Minestrone

The perfect accompaniment to a lunchtime sandwich.

1   15-ounce can navy beans, drained
1   cup shredded cabbage
½   cup sliced carrot
½   cup sliced celery
½   cup chopped onion
2   tablespoons snipped parsley
1   clove garlic, minced
1   16-ounce can tomatoes, cut up
1   10½-ounce can condensed beef broth
1½   teaspoons dried basil, crushed
¼   teaspoon dried oregano, crushed
1   9-ounce package frozen Italian green beans
2   ounces spaghetti, broken into 1-inch pieces (½ cup)
   Grated Parmesan cheese

● In a 3½-, 4-, 5-, or 6-quart crockery cooker place navy beans, cabbage, carrot, celery, onion, parsley, and garlic. Stir in *undrained* tomatoes, beef broth, basil, oregano, 3 cups *water,* and ¼ teaspoon *pepper.* Cover; cook on low-heat setting for 9 to 11 hours or on high-heat setting for 4 to 5 hours.

● Rinse green beans under running water to separate. Stir green beans and spaghetti into soup mixture. Cover; cook on low-heat or high-heat setting for 1 hour more. Ladle into soup bowls. Sprinkle each serving with Parmesan cheese. Makes 8 side-dish servings.

For 1-quart crockery cooker: Omit cabbage, celery, and green beans. Use *half of a 15-ounce can (¾ cup)* navy beans, drained; *¼ cup* sliced carrot; *¼ cup* chopped onion; *1 tablespoon* snipped parsley; *1 small clove* garlic, minced; *one 7½-ounce can* tomatoes, cut up; *half of a 10½-ounce can (⅔ cup)* condensed beef broth; *¾ teaspoon* dried basil, crushed; *⅛ teaspoon* dried oregano, crushed; *¾ cup water;* and *⅛ teaspoon pepper.* Prepare as above. Cook for 9 to 11 hours. Stir in *¼ cup* broken spaghetti. Cook 1 hour more. Serve with Parmesan cheese. Serves 2.

Potato-Cheese Soup

6   medium potatoes, peeled and chopped (6 cups)
2½   cups water
½   cup chopped onion
2   teaspoons instant chicken bouillon granules
¼   teaspoon pepper
1½   cups shredded American cheese (6 ounces)
1   12-ounce can (1½ cups) evaporated milk

● In a 3½- or 4-quart crockery cooker combine potatoes, water, onion, bouillon granules, and pepper. Cover; cook on low-heat setting for 9 to 11 hours or on high-heat setting 4 to 4½ hours.

● Stir cheese and milk into soup. Cover; cook on low-heat setting for 1 hour more or on high-heat setting for 30 minutes more. Mash potatoes slightly. Makes 6 to 8 side-dish servings.

For 5- or 6-quart crockery cooker: Use *8 medium* potatoes, peeled and chopped; *4 cups* water; *¾ cup* chopped onion; *1 tablespoon* instant chicken bouillon granules; *¼ teaspoon* pepper; *2 cups* shredded American cheese (8 ounces); and *one 12-ounce can* evaporated milk plus *one 5-ounce can* evaporated milk. Prepare as above. Makes 9 to 12 side-dish servings.

For 1-quart crockery cooker: Use *2 medium* potatoes, peeled and chopped; *¾ cup* water; *¼ cup* chopped onion; *¾ teaspoon* instant chicken bouillon granules; and *dash* pepper. Prepare as above. Cook for 8 to 9 hours. Stir in *½ cup* shredded American cheese and *½ cup* evaporated milk. Cook 1 hour more. Serves 2.

THE REST OF THE MEAL

When your menu features a main dish from the oven or the grill, put your crockery cooker to work baking custards and desserts, steaming breads, or simmering vegetable dishes.

The-Rest-of-the-Meal Tips

Using Your Cooker As an Oven

For your holiday dinner, when the oven is full and all the burners on the range-top are in use, pull out your crockery cooker for festive and delicious desserts. Once tried, the Holiday Carrot Pudding, page 70, and Traditional Mincemeat, page 72, are bound to become holiday traditions at your house.

For still other ways to use your crockery cooker as an oven, turn to the baked bread and vegetable recipes in this chapter. The convenience and energy savings might just convince you to bake in your crockery cooker often.

Choose your crockery cooker, too, when you're preparing for potlucks and cookouts. Many of our crockery-baked dishes, like the baked beans, opposite, and the Fruit Compote, page 67, can be left in the cooker for handy and warm transport.

Using Your Cooker For Steaming

Before preparing any of the steamed bread or pudding recipes in this chapter, check your mold, dish, or jars to be sure they are not too tall or too wide to fit into the liner of your crockery cooker (the liner is always in place when you are cooking).

If you like, buy the specially shaped molds available in the housewares sections of department stores or at kitchen shops, or directly from crockery-cooker manufacturers.

Do not use shortening cans, coffee cans, or vegetable cans. Most cans contain lead and are painted with or sealed with materials that give off toxic gases when heated.

If you use jars, use only *canning* jars; they are tempered and will withstand the heat. Choose the straight-sided canning jars with wide mouths, because otherwise it's next to impossible to get your food out.

New England Crock-Style Baked Beans

An excellent recipe to start ahead. Simmer the beans and mix the ingredients the night before, then chill the mixture.

1 pound dry navy beans *or* dry great northern beans (2⅓ cups)
8 cups cold water
1 cup chopped onion
¼ pound salt pork, diced
1 cup water
½ cup molasses
⅓ cup packed brown sugar
1 teaspoon dry mustard
¼ teaspoon pepper

● Rinse beans. In a large saucepan or Dutch oven bring 8 cups water and beans to boiling. Reduce heat; simmer, covered, for 1½ to 2 hours or till beans are tender. Drain beans.

● In a 3½- or 4-quart crockery cooker combine drained beans, onion, and diced salt pork. Add 1 cup water, molasses, brown sugar, dry mustard, and pepper.

● Cover; cook on low-heat setting for 10 to 12 hours or on high-heat setting for 5 to 6 hours. Stir before serving. Serves 6 to 8.

For 5- or 6-quart crockery cooker: Double all ingredients. Prepare as above. Makes 12 to 16 servings.

For 1-quart crockery cooker: Use *¾ cup* dry navy beans *or* great northern beans; *3 cups* water (cook in a medium saucepan); *½ cup* chopped onion; *2 ounces* salt pork, diced; *¼ cup* water; *¼ cup* molasses; *3 tablespoons* brown sugar; *½ teaspoon* dry mustard; and *⅛ teaspoon* pepper. Prepare as above. Cook for 6 to 8 hours. Makes 2 or 3 servings.

Saucy Gingery Bean Bake

These easy baked beans go great with grilled hamburgers, hot dogs, or bratwurst.

2 31-ounce cans pork and beans with tomato sauce
¾ cup finely crushed gingersnaps (10 cookies)
¾ cup catsup
¼ cup water
¼ cup molasses
1 tablespoon minced dried onion

● In a 3½-, 4-, 5-, or 6-quart crockery cooker combine pork and beans, gingersnaps, catsup, water, molasses, and onion. Mix well. Cover; cook on low-heat setting for 5 to 6 hours or on high-heat setting for 2½ to 3 hours. Makes 10 to 12 servings.

For 1-quart crockery cooker: Use *one 28-ounce can* pork and beans with tomato sauce, *⅓ cup* finely crushed gingersnaps, *⅓ cup* catsup, *2 tablespoons* water, *2 tablespoons* molasses, and *1½ teaspoons* minced dried onion. Prepare as above. Cook for 2½ to 3 hours. Makes 3 or 4 servings.

Apple-Filled Squash

The vegetable becomes the star of the meal when your menu includes this flavorful dish.

2 small acorn squash (about 1 pound each)
2 small baking apples, cored and thinly sliced
½ cup packed brown sugar
Ground cinnamon *or* ground nutmeg
Lemon juice
¼ cup raisins
¼ cup margarine *or* butter
¼ cup water
Coarsely chopped pecans (optional)

● Cut squash in half lengthwise; remove seeds. Arrange *one-fourth* of the sliced apples atop *each* squash half. Sprinkle *each* half with *2 tablespoons* of brown sugar, a dash of cinnamon or nutmeg, and a few drops of lemon juice. Top *each* half with *1 tablespoon* raisins and *1 tablespoon* margarine or butter. Wrap each squash half securely in foil.

● Pour ¼ cup water into a 3½-, 4-, 5-, or 6-quart crockery cooker with liner in place. Stack squash, cut side up, in cooker. Cover; cook on low-heat setting for 5½ to 6 hours or on high-heat setting for 4 to 4½ hours.

● Lift squash halves from cooker; remove foil. Sprinkle squash with pecans, if desired. Drain any syrup remaining in foil into a small pitcher; serve with squash. Makes 4 servings.

For 1-quart crockery cooker: Use one-fourth of all ingredients. Prepare as above. Cook for 4 to 5 hours. Makes 1 serving.

Ratatouille

A medley of summer vegetables.

1½ cups chopped onion
1 clove garlic, minced
1 tablespoon olive oil *or* cooking oil
1 6-ounce can tomato paste
1 tablespoon sugar
1 teaspoon dried basil, crushed
½ teaspoon salt
½ teaspoon dried thyme, crushed
¼ teaspoon pepper
4 medium tomatoes, peeled and coarsely chopped
2 medium zucchini, halved lengthwise and sliced
1 small eggplant, peeled and cubed (about 3 cups)

● In a saucepan cook onion and garlic in hot olive oil or cooking oil till tender but not brown.

● Meanwhile, in a 3½- or 4-quart crockery cooker combine tomato paste, sugar, basil, salt, thyme, and pepper. Add tomatoes, zucchini, and eggplant. Stir in onion mixture.

● Cover; cook on low-heat setting for 10 to 12 hours or on high-heat setting for 5 to 5½ hours. Stir before serving. Serves 8.

For 5- or 6-quart crockery cooker: Not recommended.

For 1-quart crockery cooker: Use *1 cup* chopped, peeled tomato; *1 cup* sliced zucchini; and *1 cup* cubed, peeled eggplant. Halve remaining ingredients. Prepare as above. Cook for 7 to 8 hours. Makes 4 servings.

Apple-Filled Squash

Apple Harvest Pudding

Substitute whipped cream for the hard sauce if you're short on time.

1 cup all-purpose flour
¼ cup packed brown sugar
1 teaspoon baking powder
¾ teaspoon ground cinnamon
   Dash ground nutmeg
3 tablespoons shortening
1 slightly beaten egg
⅓ cup milk
1 large apple, peeled, cored, and finely chopped
1 cup sifted powdered sugar
¼ cup butter, softened
1 egg yolk
½ teaspoon vanilla
1 stiffly beaten egg white

● In a bowl combine flour, brown sugar, baking powder, cinnamon, and nutmeg. Cut in shortening till crumbly. Combine egg and milk; add to dry ingredients, stirring just till moistened. Fold in apple. Pour into a well-greased 1-quart soufflé dish.

● Cover dish tightly with foil. Tear off two 15x6-inch pieces of *heavy* foil. Fold each piece in thirds lengthwise. Crisscross the foil strips; place the dish in the center. Lift the ends of the strips (see tip, page 17) and transfer the dish to a 3½-, 4-, 5-, or 6-quart crockery cooker with liner in place. (Leave strips under dish.) Pour warm water into the cooker around the dish to a depth of 2 inches. Cover; cook on high-heat setting about 3 hours or till a wooden toothpick inserted near the center comes out clean. Remove dish from cooker. Cool 10 minutes; unmold.

● For hard sauce, in a small mixing bowl beat together powdered sugar and butter. Beat in egg yolk and vanilla. Fold in egg white. Serve pudding warm with hard sauce. Serves 6.

For 1-quart crockery cooker: Use ½ *cup* all-purpose flour, *2 tablespoons* brown sugar, ½ *teaspoon* baking powder, ¼ *teaspoon* ground cinnamon, *dash* ground nutmeg, *1 tablespoon* shortening, *1* slightly beaten egg, *2 tablespoons* milk, and ½ *cup* finely chopped, peeled apple. Prepare as above. Pour into a well-greased *2-cup* soufflé dish; cover. Pour warm water into cooker around dish to a depth of *1 inch.* Cook for 2¼ to 2½ hours. For hard sauce, use same ingredient amounts. Serves 3.

Saucy Poached Fruit

This delicious rosy sauce goes with pears, apples, or plums.

4 medium or 6 small pears, 4 or 5 medium cooking apples, *or* 12 red plums
½ cup burgundy
¼ cup sugar
1 tablespoon lemon juice
⅛ teaspoon ground cinnamon
⅛ teaspoon ground nutmeg
2 tablespoons orange marmalade
   Soft-style cream cheese *or* dairy sour cream

● Peel fruit. Core fruit from the bottom, leaving stems on. Place fruit upright in a 3½- or 4-quart crockery cooker. In a bowl stir together burgundy, sugar, lemon juice, cinnamon, and nutmeg. Blend in marmalade. Pour burgundy mixture over fruit.

● Cover; cook on low-heat setting for 3 to 3½ hours. Serve warm or chilled with cream cheese or sour cream. Serves 4 to 6.

For 5- or 6-quart crockery cooker: Double all ingredients. Prepare as above. Makes 8 to 12 servings.

For 1-quart crockery cooker: Halve all ingredients. Prepare as above. Cook for 3 to 3½ hours. Makes 2 or 3 servings.

Orange-Pumpkin Custard

Flavored coffees and teas make dessert extra special. Try orange or cinnamon flavors with this smooth pumpkin dish.

2 slightly beaten eggs
1 cup canned pumpkin
½ cup sugar
½ teaspoon ground cinnamon
½ teaspoon finely shredded orange peel
¼ teaspoon ground allspice
1⅓ cups evaporated milk

● In a large mixing bowl combine eggs, pumpkin, sugar, cinnamon, orange peel, and allspice. Stir in milk. Pour into a 1-quart soufflé dish. Cover dish tightly with foil.

● Tear off two 15x6-inch pieces of *heavy* foil. Fold each piece in thirds lengthwise. Crisscross the strips and place the soufflé dish in the center. Lift the ends of the strips (see tip, page 17) and transfer the dish to a 3½-, 4-, 5-, or 6-quart crockery cooker with liner in place. (Leave strips under dish.) Pour warm water into the cooker around the dish to a depth of 2 inches.

● Cover cooker; cook on low-heat setting about 4 hours or on high-heat setting about 2 hours or till a knife inserted near the center comes out clean. Use the foil strips to lift the dish out of cooker. Let stand 20 minutes. Serve warm or chilled. Serves 4.

For 5- or 6-quart crockery cooker: Leave all ingredients the same. Prepare as above. Cook on low-heat setting for 4½ to 5 hours or on high-heat setting for 2¼ to 2½ hours. Serves 4.

For 1-quart crockery cooker: Halve all ingredients. Prepare as above. Pour pumpkin mixture into a *2-cup* soufflé dish. Pour warm water into the cooker around the dish to a depth of *1 inch*. Cook about 3 hours. Makes 2 or 3 servings.

Fruit Compote

Serve warm over slices of pound cake or ice cream.

2 15½-ounce cans pineapple chunks
1 8-ounce package mixed dried fruit
½ cup packed brown sugar
⅓ cup rum *or* whiskey
1 teaspoon finely shredded orange peel
½ teaspoon finely shredded lemon peel
½ cup orange juice
2 tablespoons lemon juice
1 16-ounce can pitted dark sweet cherries, drained

● In a 3½- or 4-quart crockery cooker combine *undrained* pineapple, dried fruit, brown sugar, and rum or whiskey. Stir in orange peel, lemon peel, orange juice, and lemon juice.

● Cover; cook on low-heat setting for 9 to 10 hours or on high-heat setting for 4½ to 5 hours. To serve, gently stir in drained cherries. Cover; cook on low-heat or high-heat setting for 15 minutes more. Makes 8 servings.

For 5- or 6-quart crockery cooker: Double all ingredients. Prepare as above. Makes 16 servings.

For 1-quart crockery cooker: Halve all ingredients. Prepare as above. Cook for 9 to 10 hours. Add drained cherries. Cook for 15 minutes more. Makes 4 servings.

Christmas
Bread Pudding

Christmas Bread Pudding

9 slices whole wheat bread
8 slices white bread
3 beaten egg yolks
1½ cups light cream
⅓ cup sugar
Dash salt
1½ teaspoons vanilla
⅔ cup light raisins
⅔ cup dark raisins
⅓ cup whole candied red
   cherries, halved
¾ cup cream sherry
1 cup water
2 beaten egg yolks
¼ cup sifted powdered sugar
2 tablespoons cream sherry
¼ teaspoon vanilla
½ cup whipping cream

● Remove crusts from bread; set crusts aside for another use. Cover bread slices with paper towels and let stand overnight.

● For custard, in a heavy medium saucepan combine 3 egg yolks, light cream, sugar, and salt. Cook and stir over medium heat. Continue cooking till mixture coats a metal spoon. Remove from heat; cool at once by placing saucepan in a sink of ice water and stirring for 1 to 2 minutes. Stir in 1½ teaspoons vanilla. Cover surface with clear plastic wrap.

● In a small bowl combine raisins. Place cherries in another bowl. Heat ¾ cup sherry till warm. Pour ⅔ *cup* sherry over raisins; pour remaining sherry over cherries. Set aside. Cut bread into ½-inch cubes (should have about 9 cups). In a bowl fold bread into custard till coated. Grease a 6½-cup tower mold (without tube). Drain raisins and cherries, reserving sherry.

● Arrange *one-fourth* of cherries in bottom of the mold; sprinkle ⅓ *cup* raisins into the mold. Add *one-fourth* of bread-cube mixture. Sprinkle with *2 tablespoons* reserved sherry. Repeat layers three times, arranging cherries and raisins near edges of the mold. Lightly press last layer with the back of a spoon. Pour remaining reserved sherry over all. Cover mold tightly with foil.

● Set mold into a 3½- or 4-quart crockery cooker with liner in place. Pour 1 cup water into cooker around mold. Cover; cook on low-heat setting about 5½ hours or on high-heat setting about 3 hours or till pudding springs back when touched.

● Meanwhile, for sherry sauce, in a mixing bowl combine 2 egg yolks, powdered sugar, 2 tablespoons sherry, and ¼ teaspoon vanilla. In a small mixing bowl beat whipping cream with a rotary beater till soft peaks form. Gently fold whipped cream into egg-yolk mixture. Cover and chill till serving time.

● Remove mold from cooker and let stand 10 minutes. Carefully unmold pudding onto a serving platter. Serve warm with sherry sauce. (*Or,* remove pudding from mold, cover, and chill. To serve, return pudding to the same mold. Cover with foil and place in the cooker, then pour 1 cup *water* around mold. Cover; cook on high-heat setting for 1½ to 2 hours or till warm. Let stand 10 minutes; unmold and serve with sauce.) Serves 12.

For 5- or 6-quart crockery cooker: Use 1½ cups *water* to pour around mold. Leave remaining ingredient amounts the same.

For 1-quart crockery cooker: Not recommended.

Holiday Carrot Pudding

1¼ cups all-purpose flour
1 teaspoon baking powder
½ teaspoon baking soda
½ teaspoon ground cinnamon
½ teaspoon ground nutmeg
2 eggs
¾ cup packed brown sugar
½ cup shortening
2 medium carrots, sliced
1 medium apple, peeled, cored, and cut into eighths
1 medium potato, peeled and cut into pieces
¾ cup raisins
2 tablespoons brandy
1 3-ounce package cream cheese
¼ cup margarine *or* butter
1 teaspoon vanilla
1 cup sifted powdered sugar
2 tablespoons milk

● In a large mixing bowl combine flour, baking powder, baking soda, cinnamon, and nutmeg; set aside. In a blender container or a food processor bowl place eggs, brown sugar, and shortening. Cover; blend or process till smooth. Add carrots; blend or process till chopped. Add apple; blend or process till chopped. Add potato; blend or process till finely chopped. Stir carrot mixture and raisins into dry ingredients; mix well.

● Pour batter into a greased and floured 6½-cup tower mold (without tube); cover tightly with greased foil. Set the mold into a 3½-, 4-, 5-, or 6-quart crockery cooker with liner in place. Cover; cook on high-heat setting for 4 hours. Remove mold from cooker. Cool 10 minutes. Unmold pudding; brush with brandy. Let stand 20 to 30 minutes before serving.

● For sauce, in a small bowl beat cream cheese, margarine or butter, and vanilla till light and fluffy. Slowly beat in powdered sugar. Stir in milk till smooth. Drizzle some cream-cheese sauce over pudding. Pass remaining sauce. Serves 6 to 8.

For 1-quart crockery cooker: Not recommended.

Pumpkin Bread

Serve round slices of this bread with soft-style cream cheese.

½ cup all-purpose flour
¾ teaspoon baking powder
½ teaspoon pumpkin pie spice
¼ cup packed brown sugar
1 tablespoon cooking oil
1 egg
¼ cup canned pumpkin
2 tablespoons raisins *or* dried currants, finely chopped

● In a small bowl combine flour, baking powder, and pumpkin pie spice. In a medium mixing bowl combine brown sugar and oil; beat till well combined. Beat in egg. Add pumpkin; mix well. Add flour mixture. Beat just till combined. Stir in raisins.

● Pour pumpkin mixture into 2 well-greased and floured ½-pint straight-sided canning jars. Cover jars tightly with greased foil. Place a piece of crumpled foil in a 3½- or 4-quart crockery cooker with liner in place. Place jars atop crumpled foil. Cover; cook on high-heat setting for 1½ to 1¾ hours or till a wooden toothpick inserted near the centers comes out clean.

● Remove jars from cooker; cool 10 minutes in jars. Remove bread from jars. Cool thoroughly on a wire rack. Makes 2 loaves.

For 5- or 6-quart crockery cooker: Double all ingredients and use *four* ½-pint canning jars. Prepare as above. Cook on high-heat setting for 2 to 2¼ hours. Makes 4 loaves.

For 1-quart crockery cooker: Not recommended.

Brownie Cakes

Even more delicious if you drizzle hot fudge topping over the cake and ice cream.

1 cup all-purpose flour
1 cup sugar
½ teaspoon baking soda
¼ teaspoon ground cinnamon (optional)
⅓ cup margarine *or* butter
¼ cup water
3 tablespoons unsweetened cocoa powder
¼ cup buttermilk *or* sour milk
1 beaten egg
½ teaspoon vanilla
¼ cup finely chopped walnuts
  Ice cream

● Grease two 1-pint straight-sided wide-mouth canning jars; line the bottom of each jar with waxed paper. Set aside. In a small bowl stir together flour, sugar, baking soda, and cinnamon, if desired. Set aside.

● In a medium saucepan combine margarine, water, and cocoa powder; heat and stir till margarine is melted and mixture is well blended. Remove from heat; stir in flour mixture. Add buttermilk, egg, and vanilla; beat by hand till smooth. Stir in nuts.

● Pour mixture into the prepared canning jars. Cover the jars tightly with greased foil. Place the jars in a 3½-, 4-, 5-, or 6-quart crockery cooker with liner in place. Cover; cook on high-heat setting for 2¾ to 3 hours or till cakes spring back when touched and a long wooden toothpick inserted near the centers comes out clean. Remove jars from cooker; cool 10 minutes. Unmold cakes; remove waxed paper. Serve warm or cool with ice cream. Makes 8 servings.

For 1-quart crockery cooker: Not recommended.

Using canning jars as baking molds

Create a simple baking or steaming mold with a straight-sided wide-mouth canning jar. To assure that the baked cake or bread will slip out easily, grease the inside of the jar well. Lining the bottom of the jar with waxed paper also will help.

   Cover each jar with a piece of foil greased on one side. Place the greased side *down* and press the foil around the edges to seal tightly.

Boston Brown Bread

Serve with a baked-bean casserole or a main-dish salad.

½ cup whole wheat flour
¼ cup all-purpose flour
¼ cup yellow cornmeal
½ teaspoon baking powder
¼ teaspoon baking soda
⅛ teaspoon salt
1 beaten egg
¾ cup buttermilk *or* sour milk
¼ cup molasses
2 tablespoons sugar
2 teaspoons cooking oil
2 tablespoons raisins, finely chopped
½ cup warm water

● In a mixing bowl stir together whole wheat flour, all-purpose flour, cornmeal, baking powder, soda, and salt. In a small bowl combine egg, buttermilk, molasses, sugar, and oil. Add egg mixture to flour mixture, stirring just till combined. Stir in raisins.

● Pour mixture into 2 well-greased 1-pint straight-sided wide-mouth canning jars; cover tightly with foil (see tip, page 71). Set jars in a 3½-, 4-, 5-, or 6-quart crockery cooker with liner in place. Pour ½ cup warm water into cooker around jars.

● Cover; cook on high-heat setting about 2 hours or till a wooden toothpick inserted near the centers comes out clean. Remove jars from cooker; cool 10 minutes. Carefully remove bread from jars. Cool completely on a rack before cutting. Makes 2 loaves.

For 1-quart crockery cooker: Not recommended.

Traditional Mincemeat

Use in your favorite recipes for mincemeat pie and muffins.

¾ pound boneless beef chuck *or* rump roast
2 pounds cooking apples, peeled, cored, and chopped (about 6 cups)
1¼ cups dark raisins
1¼ cups light raisins
1 cup dried currants
⅓ cup diced candied citron
⅓ cup diced mixed candied fruits and peels
2 tablespoons quick-cooking tapioca
2 tablespoons margarine *or* butter
1 cup sugar
¾ cup apple juice
½ cup dry sherry
¼ cup brandy
¼ cup molasses
2 teaspoons ground cinnamon
1 teaspoon ground nutmeg
1 teaspoon ground mace
⅛ teaspoon pepper

● Trim fat from meat; chop meat. In a 3½-, 4-, 5-, or 6-quart crockery cooker combine chopped meat, apples, dark raisins, light raisins, currants, citron, candied fruits and peels, tapioca, and margarine or butter.

● Add sugar, apple juice, sherry, brandy, molasses, cinnamon, nutmeg, mace, and pepper. Stir well. Cover; cook on low-heat setting for 10 to 12 hours or on high-heat setting for 5 to 6 hours. Skim off fat.

● Divide mincemeat into 1-, 2-, or 4-cup portions. Use immediately. (*Or,* place into freezer containers. Seal and label. Freeze up to 3 months. Thaw frozen mincemeat in the refrigerator overnight before using.) Makes 8 cups mincemeat.

For 1-quart crockery cooker: Not recommended.

BEVERAGES

From hot cocoa for a family affair to alcoholic and nonalcoholic beverages for a wintertime party, let your crockery cooker help cater your next event. Television bowl games, holiday open houses, and receptions are the perfect times for crockery-cooked, serve-yourself drinks.

Party Time With Your Cooker

When it's cold and damp outside, greet your guests with the aroma of spiced punch simmering in your crockery cooker.

On the low-heat setting, your hot beverage will stay a perfect sipping temperature throughout the evening. And because your guests can serve themselves from the cooker, you'll save on replenishing trips back and forth to the range-top.

The same is true if you use your crockery cooker for serving dips and appetizers, such as the Cocktail Turkey Meatballs, below. The smaller 1-quart crockery cookers, in fact, are ideal for keeping hot dips the right consistency and temperature for several hours. To serve large quantities of appetizers, you also can use 3½- or 4-quart crockery cookers.

Cocktail Turkey Meatballs

1 13-ounce bottle barbecue sauce (1¼ cups)
1 10-ounce jar apple jelly
4 teaspoons quick-cooking tapioca
1 tablespoon vinegar
1 beaten egg
¼ cup fine dry seasoned bread crumbs
2 tablespoons milk
¼ teaspoon garlic salt
1 pound ground raw turkey
   Nonstick spray coating

● In a 3½- or 4-quart crockery cooker stir together barbecue sauce, jelly, tapioca, and vinegar. Cover; cook on high-heat setting while preparing meatballs.

● For meatballs, in a large bowl combine egg, bread crumbs, milk, and garlic salt. Add ground turkey and mix well. Shape into ½- to ¾-inch meatballs. Spray a 12-inch skillet with non-stick coating; add meatballs and brown on all sides over medium heat. Drain meatballs.

● Add meatballs to crockery cooker; stir gently. Cover; cook on high-heat setting for 1½ to 2 hours. Serve immediately or keep warm on low-heat setting up to 2 hours. Makes 30 meatballs.

For 5- or 6-quart crockery cooker: Double all ingredients. Prepare as above. Makes 60 meatballs.

For 1-quart crockery cooker: Use ¾ *cup* barbecue sauce, ¾ *cup* apple jelly, *1 tablespoon* quick-cooking tapioca, *1 tablespoon* vinegar, *1* beaten egg, *3 tablespoons* fine dry seasoned bread crumbs, *1 tablespoon* milk, *⅛ teaspoon* garlic salt, *¾ pound* ground raw turkey, and nonstick spray coating. Prepare as above. Cook for 3 to 4 hours. Makes 24 meatballs.

Hot-and-Spicy Cranberry Punch

For a nonalcoholic punch, substitute 2½ cups white grape juice for the red wine and cranberry liqueur, and omit the honey. (Pictured on page 77.)

4 whole cardamom pods
8 inches stick cinnamon, broken
6 whole cloves
2 cups dry red wine
1⅓ cups water
1 6-ounce can frozen cranberry juice concentrate
3 tablespoons honey
½ cup cranberry liqueur *or* crème de cassis (optional)
Orange slices, halved (optional)
Whole cloves (optional)

● Pinch cardamom pods to break open. Tie cardamom, cinnamon, and 6 whole cloves in a spice bag (see tip, page 78).

● In a 3½- or 4-quart crockery cooker combine spice bag, wine, water, frozen juice concentrate, and honey. Add cranberry liqueur or crème de cassis, if desired. Cover; cook on low-heat setting for 4 to 6 hours or on high-heat setting for 2 to 2½ hours.

● Remove and discard spice bag. If desired, stud orange slices with additional whole cloves (see photo, page 77). Ladle punch into cups and float an orange slice atop each serving. Makes 9 (4-ounce) servings.

For 5- or 6-quart crockery cooker: Double all ingredients. Prepare as above. Cook on low-heat setting for 6 to 8 hours or on high-heat setting 4 to 5 hours. Makes 18 (4-ounce) servings.

For 1-quart crockery cooker: Halve all ingredients. Prepare as above. Cook for 3½ to 4 hours. Makes 4 (4-ounce) servings.

Honey-Mulled Apple Juice

Choose either honey or brown sugar to sweeten the drink.

6 inches stick cinnamon, broken
1 teaspoon whole allspice
1 teaspoon whole cloves
10 cups apple juice (2½ quarts)
⅓ cup honey *or* packed brown sugar
Cinnamon sticks (optional)

● Tie broken stick cinnamon, allspice, and cloves in a spice bag (see tip, page 78). In a 3½-, 4-, 5-, or 6-quart crockery cooker combine spice bag, apple juice, and honey or brown sugar.

● Cover; cook on low-heat setting for 5 to 6 hours or on high-heat setting for 2½ to 3 hours.

● Remove spice bag and discard. Serve in mugs with a cinnamon-stick stirrer, if desired. Makes 10 (8-ounce) servings.

For 1-quart crockery cooker: Use *2 inches* stick cinnamon, broken; *¼ teaspoon* whole allspice; *¼ teaspoon* whole cloves; *3 cups* apple juice; and *2 tablespoons* honey *or* brown sugar. Prepare as above. Cook for 3½ to 4 hours. Serves 3.

Crockery Cocoa

Make it spicy by adding 1 teaspoon ground cinnamon and ⅛ teaspoon ground nutmeg with the dry milk. Make it mocha-style by stirring ¾ teaspoon instant coffee crystals into each serving.

3½ cups nonfat dry milk powder
½ cup sugar
½ cup unsweetened cocoa
   powder
6 cups water
1 teaspoon vanilla
   Marshmallows (optional)
   Ground cinnamon (optional)

● In a 3½-, 4-, 5-, or 6-quart crockery cooker combine dry milk powder, sugar, and cocoa powder. Add water and vanilla; stir well to dissolve. Cover; cook on low-heat setting for 3 to 4 hours or on high-heat setting for 1 to 1½ hours.

● Before serving, carefully beat cocoa with a rotary beater to make it frothy. Ladle into mugs; top with marshmallows and sprinkle with cinnamon, if desired. Makes 9 (6-ounce) servings.

For 1-quart crockery cooker: Halve all ingredients. Prepare as above. Cook for 3 hours. Serves 4 or 5.

Hot Buttered Apple Rum

4 inches stick cinnamon,
   broken
1 teaspoon whole allspice
1 teaspoon whole cloves
7 cups apple juice
1 to 1½ cups rum
⅓ cup packed brown sugar
   Butter *or* margarine

● Tie cinnamon, allspice, and cloves in a spice bag (see tip, page 78). In a 3½-, 4-, 5-, or 6-quart crockery cooker combine spice bag, apple juice, rum, and brown sugar. Cover; cook on low-heat setting for 7 to 8 hours or on high-heat setting for 3 to 4 hours.

● Discard spice bag. Ladle hot punch into cups; float about ½ *teaspoon* butter or margarine atop each serving. Makes 10 (6-ounce) servings.

For 1-quart crockery cooker: Use *1 inch* stick cinnamon, ¼ *teaspoon* whole allspice, ¼ *teaspoon* whole cloves, *2 cups* apple juice, ¼ *cup* rum, *4 teaspoons* brown sugar, and butter or margarine. Prepare as above. Cook for 3½ to 7 hours. Serves 3.

Touchdown Toddy

A mellow drink for fall and winter afternoons.

16 whole cloves
4 inches stick cinnamon,
   broken
6 cups apple juice
4 cups water
1 cup burgundy
⅔ cup instant lemon-flavored
   tea powder

● Tie cloves and cinnamon in a spice bag (see tip, page 78). In a 3½-, 4-, 5-, or 6-quart crockery cooker combine spice bag, apple juice, water, burgundy, and tea powder. Cover; cook on low-heat setting for 4 to 6 hours or on high-heat setting for 3 to 4 hours. Discard spice bag. Makes 11 (8-ounce) servings.

For 1-quart crockery cooker: Use *4* whole cloves; *1½ inches* stick cinnamon, broken; *2 cups* apple juice; *1 cup* water; ⅓ *cup* burgundy; and ¼ *cup* instant lemon-flavored tea powder. Prepare as above. Cook for 3 hours. Serves 3 or 4.

Crockery Cocoa

Hot-and-Spicy Cranberry Punch
(see recipe, page 75)

Hot Buttered
Apple Rum

Spicy Surprise Sipper

You'll be surprised by the delicious blend that results from this unusual combination of fruit juices, beer, and vodka or rum.

Peel of 1 lemon, cut into
   strips
5 inches stick cinnamon,
   broken
1 teaspoon whole allspice
1 teaspoon whole cloves
4 cups water
1 12-ounce can frozen
   pineapple-orange juice
   concentrate
¼ cup honey
2 12-ounce cans beer
½ cup vodka *or* rum

● Tie lemon peel, stick cinnamon, allspice, and cloves in a spice bag. In a 3½-, 4-, 5-, or 6-quart crockery cooker combine spice bag, water, pineapple-orange juice concentrate, and honey. Stir in beer and vodka or rum.

● Cover; cook on low-heat setting for 4 to 6 hours or on high-heat setting for 2 to 3 hours. Remove and discard spice bag. Makes 12 (6-ounce) servings.

For 1-quart crockery cooker: Use peel of *half* of a lemon, cut into strips; *3 inches* stick cinnamon, broken; *½ teaspoon* whole allspice; *½ teaspoon* whole cloves; *2 cups* water; *one 6-ounce can* frozen pineapple-orange juice concentrate; *2 tablespoons* honey; *1 cup* beer; and *¼ cup* vodka *or* rum. Prepare as above. Cook for 2 to 3 hours. Makes about 5 (6-ounce) servings.

Making a spice bag
Removing the whole spices and fruit peel from a mixture is quick when you have them bundled together.

   Cut a double thickness of cheesecloth into a 6- or 8-inch square. Then place the whole spices and peels in the center. Bring up the corners of the cheesecloth and tie them with a clean string.

Index

Index

For even more ways to get dinner ready easily, turn to BETTER HOMES AND GARDENS® *20 Minutes to Dinner* and *In-a-Hurry Cook Book.* Each book is packed with recipes sure to fit your busy schedule.